Nothing Is Wasted

A True Story of
Finding Peace in Chaos

LORE COTTONE

ISBN 978-1-63525-386-3 (Paperback)
ISBN 978-1-63525-387-0 (Digital)

Christian Faith Publishing, Inc.
296 Chestnut Street
Meadville, PA 16335
www.christianfaithpublishing.com

Printed in the United States of America

CONTENTS

To my Savior, Jesus Christ

We have an amazingly powerful and loving God!

ACKNOWLEDGEMENTS

Thank you, Graham, for allowing me to tell this story. I am truly in awe of you. You are a strong, brilliant, creative, resilient, funny, and loving person. I am so proud to call you my son. God has made wonderful life changes in me because of you. Thank you for allowing me to tell our story. I know it is because of your desire to see God glorified that you have mustered the courage to sit back and watch parts of your story be told. Thank you for being patient with the process as our memories of some details were not always the same.

Graham and I have discussed how our memories differ on many details. I trust the reader understands this book is based totally on my recollection of the details. Graham has plans to author his own book soon, telling you his recollection of the details, plus many more stories that I have not been privy to as of yet. I can't wait to read *your* book, Graham.

Thank you, my wonderful husband, Michael. You are God's gift to me. You have always pointed me to my Jesus. We make a great team and really beautiful babies.

There are no words enough to say how very grateful I am to all my dear friends. I can't possibly mention you all by name. You know who you are. All my church friends and all my wonderful brothers and sisters from the SAPRC who walked through the worst of this journey with me. You prayed with me and for Graham. You cried and laughed with me. You grieved and rejoiced with me. You encouraged me and held me up in troubled times. God's family is the *best*!

Here's a special shout-out and thanks to Wayne and Jayne Bost, who allowed me to stay in their beautiful mountain home to write in peace; Suzanne Zucca, who proofread and edited my writing (you are extremely talented, and I'm so grateful); Milena Christopher, a godly attorney who gave me much-needed legal advice; Andrea Pettis, my gracious friend and website designer (www.lorecottone.com); Peter and Walt and their entire crew at www.movingworks.org, who produced a most excellent video depicting our testimony; and *all* my friends and family for believing in me and encouraging me to get this book written.

To God be the glory!

The Beginning of a Journey

The three younger boys were playing outside as my husband, Michael, hammered away in his workshop. The sun was shining bright and warm, and as was typical for this time of year, my boys were running around outside, dodging trees and yelling in their cutoff shorts and bare feet. Because the soil was very rocky where we lived, most people were impressed with my sons' ability to endure the harshness of the earth. They all had calloused feet and were as brown as biscuits, as we say in the South. As usual, I was busy making sure the boys were playing nicely. Our eleven-year-old son, Graham, was at his friend's house. Jake, Titus, and Blake—ten, eight, and six years old respectively—were playing in the yard. The boys were riding their bikes and skateboards, making ramps to jump. While I was outside, I decided to go into the garage and look in the chest freezer to see if there was any food I had forgotten. The garage was detached from the house, so I rarely made my way out there except to get in the car. We had bought the freezer some time before with the intention of purchasing half a cow and storing the meat. It sounded like a great idea at the time. Though we had owned the freezer for a couple of years, we had yet to purchase the cow, so the freezer was rarely used.

I walked over to the freezer, opened it, and was stunned by the great surprise it held. I am using the word *great* to imply the size, not the quality of the surprise. The entire freezer was filled with water, all 17.5 cubic feet. We were now owners of the largest ice cube known to man.

"BOYS !" They had heard this panicked tone from their mother on many occasions. As you can imagine, four boys can require this tone and volume often. I remember Jake running over to me and telling me Graham had filled it up with water a long time ago. Graham had this grand idea of riding a large cube of ice all the way down the driveway. I wondered for a split second how he thought he would get the ice out of the freezer in one piece, let alone to the top of the driveway in order to ride it. Then I thought, *How will we get the ice out? Will the freezer be broken?*

Although I was surprised to see the freezer full of water, I really should not have been shocked. Graham was a young boy of constant experimentation. He was a scientist at heart. From the moment he became mobile, he was taking things apart and mixing concoctions to discover what might happen. Graham broke many of our gadgets around the house, attempting to find out how they worked. He made messes in the kitchen trying a new chemical experiment or recipe he had seen on TV. It was a difficult job keeping up with Graham and his curiosity, let alone Graham and his three brothers.

I do look back at the raising of my boys, and I wish I had laughed more instead of reacting with anger. As I stood there that day, looking at that giant block of ice, I could have thought, *How creative of my son.* Instead, my blood boiled with anger as I worried about how we were going to fix the problem and whether it would cost us a new freezer or not. Since Graham wasn't there for me to yell at, I settled for Jake.

"Jake, why didn't you tell us Graham did this? You have to tell me when Graham does these things!"

Jake stood there for a second, blinking sheepishly, then said, "Mom, I think there is something else I need to tell you."

I braced myself and demanded to know his secret. Jake proceeded to tell me of a hole Graham had cut in the wall of his bedroom that was connected to our attic. Michael and I had turned some of our attic space into a private room for Graham. He needed a place of his own. He didn't fall asleep easily, so sharing a room with his brother hindered brother's sleep too. Pieces and parts of computers that Graham had taken apart always covered the floor of his room, which inhibited his brother from having any space of his own. Having a room to himself seemed like the best thing for Graham, for his brothers, and for keeping peace in the household. The house was perfect for this addition. Because of the steep pitch of the roof, Michael was able to build a normal-size staircase up to a full-size bedroom on the third story.

I ran up the two flights of stairs to assess the damage. After cutting a trail through all the junk on the ground, I made it to the side of the room where Jake had directed me. Behind his dresser, Graham had cut a hole in the dry wall in order to access the attic. I managed to contort myself and crawl inside the small entrance to find an old microwave that had been stored in the garage, some paper plates, and food.

"That's where those pickles went!" I exclaimed. I also found popcorn, chips, and Kool-Aid. I knew I had bought these items from the grocery store. I wasn't crazy after all. Now I had discovered where they went. Graham had been making himself a hideaway in the attic. He had his own room. Why did he need a hideaway? The most dangerous discovery was the spliced electrical wires Graham had cut in order to create a plug for the microwave. The most puzzling surprise we found in the attic was a horse trough. Graham was only eleven years old at the time. In order to get this trough into the attic, he had to have hauled it up there when we were all at one of the boys' football games. Graham hated football. He hated sports of any kind, really. His brothers' football games were the one time we allowed him to stay home alone. He must have carried that heavy trough up the attic stairs and over floor joists (without a floor) to get it to his place. The thought of this treacherous task frightened me. We could have come home to see Graham had fallen through the ceiling to his death. We could have had our house burn down from an electrical fire. All the what-ifs were scary thoughts. This is just one example of a random day with our young boys.

Daily devotions with the boys.

Being the mom of four boys has never been boring. When my husband, Michael, and I were married, I was twenty-seven, and he was thirty-two. We had both become believers in Jesus Christ when we were young. We watched many in our church family have five or more children, and we couldn't wait to have our own. Psalms 127:3–5 speaks of children being a blessing from God: "Blessed is the man whose quiver is full of them." A quiver is where the hunter stores his arrows, and it is full with five arrows. We felt well equipped to raise several children; in fact, we were planning on having five children, until we had four. We felt pretty full at four. As I look back now, I realize we had no idea what the future would hold for us. I now believe God grows us and equips us to parent as we go. I also wasn't prepared for how unique each individual boy would be. I'm convinced God instilled in each one a sense of adventure and a need to conquer, and they express that in different ways. Michael and I always said, "We are raising men, not boys." To me, that meant I couldn't baby them, or I would risk squelching what God had put in them. God was calling each of them to be warriors in His kingdom. What we failed to understand before we started this adventure was that we as parents were entering a war too. This was going to be a war for their souls.

There are many more stories not unlike the giant ice cube and the attic hideaway. Some stories were hilarious at the time. Some stories are funny now that time has healed the fear and anger of the moment. I am also sure there are many more stories of which I am completely unaware. Have you ever heard the old saying "Ignorance is bliss"? As soon as my boys read this book, they will most likely expose secrets they have held for years. I can hear them now: "Oh, Mom, you didn't know about this...." If my heart survives those conversations, maybe a second book will come out of that!

All parents can tell stories of mischief their little ones encountered. Many of us can tell numerous stories of how our teenagers barely made it out of their teens. I love listening to my three older brothers tell their childhood tales. The stories of "growing-up boy" are usually much more exciting than the ones I hear of "growing-up girl." However, sometimes the behavior of our children turns a corner from the mischief of filling a freezer with water or cutting a hole in the wall to making very bad decisions, which have consequences with lifelong effects. Sometimes our children are diagnosed with mental illness, disorders, and issues of brain chemistry, and we have to deal with those circumstances as well as we can. Sometimes others invade our children's lives with their own bad decisions; then we and our children are forced to pick up the pieces of those consequences. No matter the age of our child, we as parents want to help. We want to teach them, guide them, and rescue them.

Sometimes in the midst of teaching, guiding, and rescuing, we find ourselves needing some teaching, guiding, and rescuing of our own. The intention of this book is not really to teach or guide you. You will certainly read some things *not* to do. I've tried to be honest with you, telling the good, the bad, and the ugly. By God's grace, you may read some things that end up helping you in some way. This is simply *my* story, *my* perspective of raising *my* boys. All four of my boys—Graham, Jake, Titus, and Blake—are strong, handsome, kindhearted, and smart young men. They have all changed my life, and I couldn't imagine life without any one of them. However, I write this book as a collection of stories about one of my children in particular.

My oldest son, Graham, has traveled down roads Michael and I never dreamt for him. Some of these roads have been harrowing and frightening. He did not travel them alone, however. Michael and I have traveled with him as his dad and mom. We were not always physically there, but emotionally speaking, we were always there. My friends have traveled along with me via my storytelling. They've seen me break down, and they've seen me be strong. They've seen me make mistakes, and they've seen me make good decisions. They've seen me lacking faith, and they've seen me living faith. It is because of their encouragement that I write this book. My hope is that I will help some parent somewhere to understand that they are not alone. I hope to encourage parents to keep their faith along the journey. Everyone's journey is different. Mostly I aim to give glory to my Lord and Savior Jesus Christ for the life and light He has given to my family. God is always bigger than we can ever imagine. God always knows what we need. God always cares, even when we don't feel it. God travels our journey along with us.

This is my story of being mom to Graham Cottone. It is a story of failure and a story of triumph. This is how God has used Graham to change my life forever and for the better.

CHAPTER 1

The Diagnosis

When our first child was born, Michael and I were thrilled. Michael Graham was born just ten months after we were married. Our expectations were that we were going to be the best parents ever. We were pretty sure we had it all figured out before our first was born. We would name him *Graham* after my mother's family. Graham was going to be the firstborn of several siblings. We were going to teach him about Jesus early. Graham would grow up to be a kind, strong man who loved his family and his God. He would play sports, go to college, marry a beautiful young lady, and produce amazing grandchildren for us. Yep, we had it all figured out. What we didn't count on was the bumpy road complete with potholes, ditches, detours, and maybe even some sinkholes along the way.

As a baby, Graham was affectionate and happy. I did notice that he was fairly intense—he was not a mellow baby by any stretch of the imagination. He would let you know immediately and emphatically if he didn't like something. Once Graham began walking, we noticed a very interesting ritual he would engage in after every nap or night's sleep. He would run into the living room, stopping suddenly to look around the room for something to catch his eye. It was as if he were scanning the room for something out of place. If he noticed something different, he would make a beeline to it as quickly as possible. This didn't concern us. We thought of it as a sign of intelligence and curiosity. Graham stopped napping at two years old; this was not in our plan. He was quick to grab for things, he put everything in his mouth, and he was the master of severe and sometimes frightening temper tantrums. When angry, he would throw himself on the ground and bang his head on the floor. Even if it was a concrete floor, he would proceed to bang his head. I would see the fit coming and dive from wherever I was in the room in order to catch his head just before it hit the ground. After several months of this, I realized my "rescuing" him from hurting his head was only prolonging his banging. *He will never learn to stop if he doesn't know it hurts*, I told myself.

Soon after this revelation, Graham had a fit. This time, I knelt close by and cringed as he brought his head up and then down on the hard linoleum floor. His head hit hard. As he brought his head back up, Graham's eyes got big. He looked straight at me as if to ask, *What just happened?* Then he proceeded to scream. I'm not recommending this, but that was the last time Graham banged his head for a while. Later, he would still bang occasionally, but he was more selective of the surface that he allowed his head to hit. Now he was partial to choosing a wall or a carpeted area.

The first real confirmation for me that Graham was more active than most kids was when the teacher at his Mother's Day Out group pulled me aside to inform me that they couldn't continue to have Graham in their class. He was way too disruptive, and he wouldn't nap. I was embarrassed. Whose child gets kicked out of Mother's Day Out at two years of age? Michael and I sought out advice from parents of older and multiple children. The advice we received was that we needed to be more consistent with our discipline. By now, Graham had a younger brother, and life was busier. I wouldn't dare go anywhere in public with my two children without my husband or my good friend Jennifer. Someone needed to hold Graham's hand at all times, or he would run directly into traffic. Graham was extremely impulsive.

When I was pregnant with my and Michael's third child, Jennifer and I were shopping at the local outlet mall. For the sake of conversation, I mentioned how crazy it would be if I had twins. I'll never forget Jennifer saying, "If you have twins, Lore, I can't be your friend anymore." We laughed and laughed, but the truth was that Graham already felt like two in one.

Michael and I did our best to take more time in teaching Graham. I created a book for Graham with pictures of children running and grabbing as opposed to walking and waiting. We role-played situations with obedient actions. Michael and I focused our attention on helping Graham learn obedience. The next year, I took Graham back to Mother's Day Out. He was a year older, and we were being much more consistent with our discipline. I told myself he would do fine this year. After a few weeks, they pulled me aside again. "Mrs. Cottone, the trouble with Graham is that he just wants me all to himself," said his sweet teacher. That was her kind way of saying, *This boy is a handful that is too much for us*. Then she asked me if I had thought of having Graham tested for attention-deficit/hyperactivity disorder (ADHD). As we walked to the car that day, I felt like a failure. I buckled Graham into his car seat and cried all the way home. This was not in my plan.

I remember that it was at this point when I began to hear unsolicited advice at every turn. Some talked with me about changing our diet. Some were in the vitamin business and swore they had the answer that would turn Graham around. Others tried to convince us that if we would be stricter and more consistent at discipline, he would not behave this way. Our first action was to listen to the Mom's Day Out teacher. We took Graham to the doctor to be evaluated. We wanted to find out if there was a physical or neurological reason for his behavior.

At four years of age, Graham was tested, and the doctor determined he indeed had ADHD. Reluctantly, we agreed with the doctor and began giving Graham a stimulant medication on a daily basis. Because of his diagnosis, the public school system accepted Graham for enrollment at four years of age. He did well in school; the medication calmed him down. We were convinced that if medication helped Graham calm down, then it must be necessary for helping him learn and be more socially appropriate. If nothing else, Graham being on this medication helped me to cope. As Graham aged, we began to see his love of reading and his love of computers blossom. By the time he was in the third grade, Graham would devour a long book in two days. If he wasn't reading a book, he was on a computer or even taking a computer apart. Graham was intensely inquisitive. He just had to know how everything worked. If we had allowed it, Graham would have taken apart every electronic gadget we owned. His room was littered with computer parts. When I say *littered*, I mean you couldn't see the floor for all the parts, broken pieces, screws, and batteries.

Something else we noticed early on was Graham's sensitivity. He was highly tactile and often bothered by certain aspects of physical touch. Eventually he never wore jeans or anything with a tag, because he couldn't stand any stiff clothing "poking" him. But the most obvious sensitivity he had was with his hearing. If anyone made a smacking sound with their mouth while they were eating, Graham would throw an instant fit. No medication could help this. Small sounds that no one else noticed irritated him beyond the breaking point. He had to leave his classroom one day because he said the computer at the back of the room was humming so loudly he wanted to break it. No one else heard the hum.

While Graham's capacity for sensory overload was off the charts, his emotional and social sensitivities seemed stunted. Graham's lack of social awareness was something the doctor never addressed. Actually, no one had ever been able to pinpoint exactly what was happening and address this concern of mine. In fact, I remember asking our pastor's wife when Graham was very young, "How does one teach compassion?" She looked at me in a puzzled manner and answered, "I think that is something only the Holy Spirit can teach." I remember thinking, *Thanks a lot. He better hurry up because He's not doing such a great job.*

Graham responded to situations in extreme ways regardless of anyone else's feelings. I was convinced that he would impact the world in an extreme way. I constantly struggled to figure out how to mold Graham in the direction he should go. During his preschool years at the Mom's Day Out program, Graham didn't play with the other kids on the playground. He was content to spin in the tire swing alone or play by himself in the sand. When we did have one-on-one playdates, Graham's idea of engaging in play was to physically tackle the other little boy. He wasn't trying to be aggressive or harmful. He honestly acted as if he didn't understand how to engage in play. At the time, all these things seemed like merely childish behaviors he would eventually outgrow. We didn't know that these things might be signs of something else. As he grew older, Graham struggled to interact with his schoolmates, and he was not well received. He did manage to maintain one friend at a time. By the time, Graham was in the fourth grade at ten years old. He had not grown out of most of these behaviors, and we became even more gravely concerned that we were missing something important.

Graham had been on ADHD medication for six years, and he was only ten years old. I knew he did better in school with his medication. Deep down, I also thought it was easier for me to deal with Graham when he was on his medication. In my heart, my preference was actually that none of my children would ever be on medication, but in Graham's case, it seemed so necessary. On the negative side, the medicine mellowed him to the point that sometimes he did not act like himself, and I didn't like that part at all. Without the medication, though, he couldn't focus in school. He got into more fights with his brothers, and he argued more with me and Michael. I was convinced that his medication was helping Graham fit in with his peers, accomplish his studies, and stay calm at home.

When Graham was in fourth grade, I became aware that the public school would test students when the teacher or the parent requested the testing. I wasted no time—I requested full psychological testing and assessments. For years, I had said, "He may have ADHD, but we are missing something—something social." The school obliged, and they performed testing with Graham for the next several weeks. The last piece of the testing was a questionnaire for the parents. Michael and I completed the thorough questionnaire, which covered my pregnancy, all of Graham's developmental milestones, and our family life.

The psychologist then made an appointment for Michael and me to discuss her assessment. She started the meeting like all good school meetings should start, by complementing the student who had been assessed. She said Graham was so bright. She said Graham worked hard. She said it was a joy spending time with him. Then she informed us that she believed she had reached a new diagnosis for Graham. The psychologist began asking us questions like, "Did he rock or spin himself around often as a younger child?" "Did he walk on his tiptoes a lot?" "Did he ever bang his head?" By now, I was feeling a little irritated. The questions she was asking seemed to be railroading us toward a diagnosis of autism. Yes, Graham may have done those things, but not to the extent of being autistic! I suppose this line of questioning scared me a bit because I blurted out, "My child is not autistic. He can speak and function very well. He's smart too." The doctor agreed with me but asked if we had ever heard of something called Asperger syndrome (AS). We had not. The psychologist gave us an article to read that explained AS in detail. Michael and I took the article home and were astonished at the similarities to Graham. This was it! AS even explained that funny little mannerism Graham had that we thought was unique. When he would get truly excited, Graham would hop on his toes rapidly while flapping his bent arms up and down. We learned that this is a ritual many AS kids perform called *flapping*. As parents, we dove into discovering what this diagnosis meant for our son's future and how we could help him. The more we learned about Asperger syndrome, the more convinced we became that Graham had it. From our perspective, it could have been called Graham's syndrome. This newfound knowledge was not devastating news to us. On the contrary, we found hope in the fact that now we could understand Graham better, and we would surely discover effective ways to intervene and help him.

Every person with AS is very different. Although Graham didn't exhibit every known AS trait, the diagnosis explained so much for us. Graham saw everything as black or white. There were never gray areas or exceptions to a rule. For instance, one day, I remember telling my four young boys that we would go to the park the next day. In the morning, however, I had a tremendous headache—I couldn't go anywhere. It was all I could do to take care of them at home while my husband was at work. When they heard I was sick, the three younger boys went on to play as usual, unaffected by the news. Graham was not so understanding. He shouted, "You said we would go to the park. If you weren't going to take us to the park, you shouldn't have said you would!" There was nothing I could say to help him understand.

Along with his tactile sensitivity, Graham didn't catch social cues either. Instead of intuitively knowing a person's emotions, Graham had to be taught how to recognize someone's feelings by their tone or facial expressions. We would show him pictures of faces and model different tones, teaching him the proper response to someone reacting in this particular way. Sports made no sense to him. Team sports were especially ridiculous to Graham; it seemed to him that everyone was speaking some secret foreign language that was entirely unknown to him. He would rather play alone or with just one person.

Graham was highly intelligent. However, by the time Graham was in fourth grade, he began to exert his stubbornness with schoolwork. He would refuse to complete his math homework. He told me he did two or three of the problems, and that should show he had learned the math, so why would he have to do twenty problems? Graham didn't care that he would receive a bad grade. If it was illogical to him, he would not do it.

This diagnosis didn't come with a medication fix. We came to believe the diagnosis wasn't a disease, just a different way of thinking and acting, a different way of filtering and seeing the world. The school now understood Graham differently as we did. We would work together in helping him understand how he was different, celebrating his uniqueness and working toward him thriving in a world that didn't see things the way he did.

CHAPTER 2

Being Different

As Graham navigated through fifth grade, he encountered a bully who physically pushed him around daily. As far as I know, Graham never once physically defended himself. He didn't know if he should defend himself or why he needed to, much less how to defend himself. It was during this time that I overheard Graham talking in a very demeaning manner to another child. When I corrected him, he was very confused. He looked at me with hurt in his eyes and said, "If that's wrong, then why do all the kids talk to me like that at school?" My heart broke, and I wanted to take him away from that pain.

The day soon came that convinced me that Graham processed everything differently from most of his peers, and he needed special attention. I was told he was being disciplined for the next week in its entirety by serving lunch detention. When the assistant principal explained the incident to me, I was livid. Graham was seeing an occupational therapist at school who saw his need to chew or constantly have something in his mouth. Because of this, she had given Graham a short rubber straw to chew on during class. The therapist failed to inform Graham's teacher. He was obeying the instructions and chewing the straw during class; however, an unintended consequence soon followed. His saliva began to drip out of the straw and onto his desk, which distracted the other students. The teacher then told Graham that he could no longer chew on the straw because of the drooling issue. Graham attempted to tie a knot at each end of the straw to appease the teacher and still chew on the straw. When he didn't cease the chewing, the teacher sent him to the principal's office for discipline. After speaking with Graham, I determined he was only trying to do what he was told, but the school did not understand him. I was concerned that going into middle school would be very difficult on Graham. I strongly felt I should homeschool him in order to protect him from social situations he was not ready for and to protect him from bullies.

Michael and I decided I would homeschool Graham starting in sixth grade. We would revisit this decision at the end of the year. At first, Graham was fine with the idea of schooling at home. However, as we started and his brothers went off to public school, Graham changed his mind. He argued with me every day; he was relentless. One morning, I left Graham at home to complete an assignment while I went to the gym. About an hour later, a friend of mine called me saying she had just picked up my twelve-year-old son from the busy highway. He was about three miles from home on a four-lane highway that ran through our town. I rushed home to find out that Graham had walked to the middle school with the intention of enrolling himself. He told me that when he arrived, he didn't go inside because he didn't know what to do, so he just turned around and started walking back home. I wanted to reenroll him in school right then—I was tired of fighting. But I believed that God wanted me to homeschool him, whether Graham wanted me to or not.

Several significant events happened for us during that time of homeschooling. One of those was Jake's eleventh birthday. The summer before Jake's birthday, Graham had turned twelve years old. Because we knew he desired independence and because we knew it would be fun, we decided to give Graham an electric scooter for his birthday. He would be able to scoot all over the neighborhood, enjoying his freedom. We lived in a gated community with several cul-de-sacs. Our home was at the very end of the neighborhood, one mile from the entrance. It provided him with lots of room and safety. And we would have peace of mind knowing he was physically capable of handling the scooter. He seemed to really like it, and he rode it daily on the neighborhood streets.

That fall, Jake turned eleven years old. Jake didn't really care about independence as much as he cared about power and speed. We decided to give him a 50-cc dirt bike for his birthday. He would not be able to ride the streets of the neighborhood, but he didn't really care about that. What Jake wanted to do was ride the dirt paths and jump ramps on our 5-acre lot. There were lots of trees to maneuver around, as well as straight pathways on which to gain some speed.

We were proud of ourselves, thinking we had made the right decision for each boy. One thing we had discovered while taking Christian parenting classes is that each child is different and needed to be parented accordingly. Our mantra with the boys became, "If you want us to treat you fairly, we must treat you differently." Somewhere along the way, we lost our understanding of what it meant to just be a little boy and how Graham might perceive our gift to his little brother compared to what we had given him on his last birthday. We were loudly and violently reminded of Graham's feelings that day.

Michael called to tell me he was almost home. He would be driving in with the dirt bike tied up and standing in the back of his truck. I called Jake and all the boys down to come see what Dad had for Jake's birthday. As soon as the truck made its turn into our driveway and the dirt bike came into view, the eruption began. Jake, Titus, and Blake erupted with pure joy, jumping and screaming. Graham, however, stood in shocked disbelief. We unloaded the dirt bike, and Michael instructed Jake how to work the throttle, shift gears, and wear his helmet. I don't remember what Graham was doing, except that he was not jumping for joy like the other boys. Looking back, I realize the struggle of homeschooling and now this birthday gift were strong reminders to Graham that he was especially different, even in his own family. Who at twelve years old can handle feeling so different? And this was the boy who saw everything in black and white. What he got for his birthday versus what his brother got. Unfair. I do wish we had thought of letting Graham in on the secret ahead of time and explaining why we were making this choice, why we had chosen the scooter especially for Graham, and why we thought the dirt bike would be better for Jake.

Jake was saddled up and ready to take his first lap when I heard Graham scream out to me. As I turned, I saw him running with a baseball bat toward our eight-feet-tall glass doors. I began yelling out to Michael as I ran to catch Graham, but I was not fast enough. Graham took the bat and smashed both our glass doors. I stood there afraid he might swing at me. Michael came running down the hill and tackled Graham to the ground to restrain him. In all the chaos, I screamed at Michael not to hurt Graham. Michael yelled for me to call the police. I ran inside, grabbed the phone, and dialed 911. My thoughts were all over the place at this point. Why was Graham so angry? Would he calm down or do more damage? Would Michael accidently hurt Graham? Then Michael would be in trouble with the law. I was afraid—afraid for Graham, afraid for Michael, afraid for our family. The 911 dispatcher said he had an officer on the way, and he wanted me to stay on the phone. I couldn't stay on the phone with him. I needed to call my pastor. We needed more than the law. We needed our church family to help us make sense of this and help bring peace back to this crazy day.

The police soon arrived, as did our pastor and his wife. The police presence calmed Graham and brought a sense of peace to us as well. One officer spoke with Graham privately as another one spoke with me and Michael. They asked if we wanted to press charges. We seriously thought about it. Maybe a night in juvenile detention would help Graham see his behavior clearly, and he would then stop fighting his family. I had seen the TV shows where they would attempt to "scare straight" the kid who had been getting into trouble at home by having them spend a weekend in jail. I thought this might be a good idea, hopefully keeping Graham from making bigger mistakes and having more dire consequences later in life. However, if we pressed charges, it would be a felony. I didn't want Graham to have serious charges on his permanent record. I just wanted him to have a realization that he was treating his entire family with contempt and disrespect. The police and our pastor and his wife stayed all afternoon. One police officer asked if we believed in corporal punishment and told us that maybe Graham needed a good, old-fashioned spanking, even at twelve years old. As the Texas officers waited outside, Michael and Graham went inside for a "trip to the woodshed." Our pastor and his wife spoke with the entire family and then prayed with us.

After everyone left and we cleaned up the glass, I apologized to Jake for his birthday being ruined. Later that evening, a very different Graham walked along the driveway with me and told me three times that he was so sorry that he had done that. After the third apology, I stopped and said, "Graham, I forgive you. You don't have to apologize anymore." I believe that was the first sincere apology I had ever received from Graham. Maybe this would be a time of revelation for him. Maybe this extreme experience would be the thing Graham looked back on and determined never to let happen again. As a result of this incident, an elder in our church, David, offered to be Graham's mentor. They began meeting every week. David was God's gift to us as parents, as well as to Graham. They genuinely enjoyed each other. Graham could freely talk with David about issues, and David could lovingly confront him in ways we couldn't. He was a welcome buffer and mediator for us.

A month later, Michael and I attended a marriage retreat where forgiveness was being discussed. We talked with an older couple who knew of our struggles with Graham. I told them all about that day that was intended to be a celebration but ended with police intervention. The husband asked me if I had apologized to Graham. "What?" I exclaimed. "Why would I do that? I did nothing wrong." All I did was try to give Jake a wonderful birthday. Then he explained to me that sometimes we don't have to do anything wrong for the other person to need to forgive us. If the other person perceived us as hurting them, then they were hurt. Michael and I needed to lead Graham into a place of forgiveness. Whether Graham had been wronged or not was not the point. The point was that Graham had to learn how to choose forgiveness. We as his parents were responsible for making sure he was brought to that fork in the road of forgiveness and unforgiveness. This suddenly made sense to me.

I couldn't wait to get home and apologize to Graham. If we had any chance of having a good relationship with him in the future, Michael and I needed to lead him in this way.

It was a beautiful moment. We apologized to Graham for not considering his feelings when we bought Jake that motorcycle. Although we had good intentions, we had hurt our son, whom we loved dearly. Then we asked if he would please choose to forgive us. He simply said yes, and life continued.

Although it seemed like an anticlimactic ending, I knew it was a big deal in the kingdom of God. This moment of realization, repentance, and forgiveness was now complete. Graham had sincerely repented. As his parents, we had also sincerely repented. Now forgiveness had been applied, and the enemy was at a disadvantage. I hoped this would be the big turning point and a positive pattern for future interactions with Graham.

Graham continued to fight being homeschooled, and the Lord helped me realize the reason for homeschooling wasn't really for Graham's protection at school. The Lord had laid on my heart that the reason He had led me to teach Graham at home was for an opportunity to build relationship with him. This was a revelation to me. Up until now, unfortunately, I had seen my children as little ones to raise in the right way, but I had failed to build the relationships and heart connections that were necessary to enable them to be whole young men. I had times when I took each one out alone with me for shopping or dinner, but it seemed more like a ritual than a heart investment.

This revelation convinced me to use more of my heart with my children.

Graham continued to fight with me, but he needed to see that I was going to obey God over giving in to his pressure, and that I would love him through it all. I began to share my heart with him more and share what God had revealed to me. This was my attempt to let him in on my relationship with Christ. It was a personal relationship that he too could have. I encouraged Graham that he was loved and seen by God. God had a plan for his life. Through Christ, God had given Graham all he needed for success. I recited to Graham who he was in Christ. He was more than a conqueror. He was a kind and compassionate person. He had wisdom and power and a sound mind because of Christ who dwelt in him. Even if Graham didn't pay attention to my encouragement, it encouraged me to hear God's Word spoken over him.

I believe in the power of praying scriptures. The specific scripture God gave me for Graham and each of my boys was Malachi 2:5–7. That scripture became this prayer: "Lord, Your covenant of life and peace is with Graham. He will revere You and stand in awe of Your name. True instruction will be found in Graham's mouth and nothing false found on his lips. Graham will walk with You in peace and uprightness and turn many from sin. For Graham's lips ought to preserve knowledge because Graham is a messenger of the Lord Almighty, and people will seek instruction from his mouth." Sometimes I seriously questioned how this would ever actually describe Graham. I decided what I couldn't understand was irrelevant. I needed to believe God could do anything.

We managed to complete the first semester of homeschooling. I wish I could say we felt so much closer after that semester. I wish I could say that our relationship changed dramatically. But honestly, all I can say is that I obeyed God, and Graham made it through the semester. I am absolutely convinced that God did accomplish something in our relationship. That semester didn't turn the tide, but I do know that without that semester, we would be different. Since I couldn't see a huge change at the time, I believed by faith. I do believe that homeschooling Graham was more for me and our relationship than it ever was for Graham's protection. God wanted me to slow down and have Graham one-on-one for a bit. God wanted me to appreciate Graham and all his differences.

His Asperger's diagnosis was not a bad thing. Graham saw the world in a different way than most people. I began to see him more as gifted and talented in a very untraditional form. Maybe there are more children diagnosed with AS now than in times past because we need these people and their gifts and talents more than ever before. Everything I learned about Graham was just the tip of the iceberg. We enrolled Graham in school for his second semester. Both Graham and I breathed a sigh of relief.

CHAPTER 3

More Pieces of the Pie

When Graham returned to school that year, he did very well. He was focused on his schoolwork and determined more than ever to prove to me that he could navigate middle school. He made good grades and even joined the student council. Graham's determination was very impressive. He did prove to me what I had never really doubted: whatever Graham put his mind to do would be accomplished. I settled back into being the mom of four boys who were all in school and doing well. Life was good, and I relaxed.

That following summer began to get progressively hard. Graham seemed to be sad and was withdrawing from the family. Family time no longer seemed like much fun but became instead very hard work emotionally. It was not uncommon for Graham to be angry with us. He wanted to be alone a lot. Since

Graham didn't enjoy *his* time with us, he wasn't going to let any of *us* enjoy our time together either. Maybe vacations were especially difficult for Graham because we were in new places, and his routine was gone. We have always been more spontaneous on vacations. Perhaps Graham had increased anxiety during these times. I know my anxiety increased because of Graham's often unpredictable behavior.

There were a few occasions when Graham would open his car door as we traveled down an interstate going sixty-five miles an hour. One of those times was while we were vacationing in Orlando, Florida, and Graham became upset about something. He wanted to get away from us, so he suddenly opened the car door, putting himself, all of us, and the other travelers going down that highway in jeopardy. Fed up with this behavior, Michael stopped the car and told him to get out. We left him there to walk. Terrified at the thought of leaving our thirteen-year-old alone on a strange highway, I argued with Michael until I finally won, and we circled around to retrieve him from the highway. Michael and I often didn't see eye to eye when it came to how to discipline Graham. Michael insisted Graham was being disrespectful and manipulative. I insisted there were many times when Graham was a victim of his AS and was screaming out for help. Looking back, I'm sure the truth lay somewhere in the middle.

Together, Michael and I navigated through the next several years as best we could. People often ask me how our marriage managed to last during all this turmoil. We did argue, often.

However, I remember one thing my husband said to me over and over again: "The most important thing here is us. We have to stay united and be a solid front. If we crumble, what will happen to the kids?" I believe that more than ever now. The best gift we can give our children is the gift of a godly marriage. All the marriage classes and retreats we attended came in handy. We had an agreement early on in the marriage that the word *divorce* was not allowed to be discussed. We were married for life, and we would not mention divorce even when things got tough.

Neither of us handled parenting perfectly. Who does? But the one thing that we knew beyond a shadow of a doubt was that we needed each other. I'm also confident that our boys need both of us. They need mom's mothering love, and they equally need a dad to call them out and father them into manhood. Sometimes that looks like a harsh push to me. I'm sure to him my mothering often seemed like I was babying them, my compassion like I was making excuses for their behavior. I think we balanced each other well in our parenting. We prayed daily together and forgave each other. God gave us Graham, so He must have known that, together, with His help, we could raise him.

As he entered his teens, Graham became increasingly unpredictable. I wondered if he might be experimenting with drugs. The truth of the situation was exposed one scary day. Michael was in the upstairs apartment over our garage with an HVAC repairman while I was in the house cooking dinner, and the kids were all playing. I walked outside to check on the crew when Michael came running out of the garage with a limp Graham in his arms. Michael was panicked, and Graham was completely unconscious. As Michael laid him on the grass, Graham woke up and asked what was going on. I was wondering the same thing. Michael began to ask Graham what he was doing in the back room of the garage. "The propane was turned on and the room shut when I found you unconscious on the floor!"

Graham had no reply except, "I don't know." He just clammed up and wouldn't talk with us about it. He proceeded to rise to his feet and walk away. If we hadn't had the repairman out when we did, we might have lost Graham that day. While looking at the AC, the repairman told Michael he smelled propane gas. Michael followed the odor to the back room of the garage. When he opened the door, he saw Graham passed out on the floor with a propane tank beside him. This was a strong wake-up call for us. We needed to discover what was going on in Graham's mind. Huffing propane was not anything we had ever heard of before, but we soon became aware of a culture of abusing petroleum inhalants among adolescents, especially boys. This type of drug abuse could take his life or, at the very least, kill brain cells permanently. I began to probe in hopes of discovering what Graham was doing that day with the propane. Was this his first time doing this? Was this intentional? Did he hope to actually end his life or just obtain a high? I talked with him, his teachers, his brothers. I searched his room. This is when I discovered he was also stealing and consuming cough medication in order to get a high. He didn't want to end his life. He needed to escape his anxiety. He was engaging in self-medication of the most dangerous kind.

Anxiety is a by-product of AS, so I was determined to find a specialist in Asperger syndrome. I managed to find a doctor in our state whose specialty was children with AS. I was overjoyed and so grateful to discover this doctor was only an hour's drive away from our home. This is when I began to see raising Graham as more of a journey than finding that one thing that would turn him around. We needed the whole journey. Graham needed David, the church mentor. He needed the time in homeschool, the public school time, and now he needed a specialist. I now saw all these interventions as a giant pie. I was grateful for all the pieces of the pie. As each piece was added, however, I did hope it was the piece to complete the pie. Maybe the specialist was that last pie piece.

Graham's new doctor was impressive. Her own daughter had Asperger syndrome, which helped add to her credibility. She explained how a child with AS can have such high anxiety that they live in a constant state of fight or flight. This is where someone is brought to a point in their anxiety or fright that they must suddenly choose if they will stand to fight or rise to flee a situation. It's known as hyperarousal, or the acute stress response. This was eye-opening for me and helped me better understand Graham. I developed more compassion for his feelings than frustration with his actions. She prescribed Graham with an antianxiety medication. I also thought maybe the medication he had taken since he was four was not as effective as it once had been. We decided to try a nonstimulant drug for ADHD.

Soon after starting this medication, Graham's attitude became much worse. He was angry all the time. He was belligerent and couldn't get along with anyone in the family. He began to fall behind in schoolwork and refused to take his ADHD medication. Graham said he hated the way he felt when he took them. I insisted he take them. I was afraid of him failing school. I didn't have the answers. We tried different schools, different doctors, different medications. I just wanted God to answer my prayers and for Graham to suddenly straighten up. I was tired of this journey. During this time, we found a therapist for him as well, but that didn't seem to help much either.

I was not terribly surprised when one day, the school called to tell me Graham had been arrested. He had taken some of his ADHD medication to school and handed it to another student. This was witnessed by a teacher, who immediately took him to the office. The school's zero-tolerance drug policy required a call to the police. Graham was thirteen years old in seventh grade, and he now had a juvenile record for distributing drugs on campus. It turns out the other kid had befriended Graham and asked him for some of his medication. Graham reacted out of his brokenness. His constant desire to fit in socially made him more than happy to comply in order to make a new friend. He spent the night in jail and received probation. The court was not interested in why he did what he did. They didn't care that he had Asperger syndrome and that his intention was to make friends. He never intended to sell or distribute drugs. My hope throughout this ordeal was that he would be scared straight.

For the next year, Graham was on probation, which made him think twice before making a bad decision. There continued to be a constant tug-of-war between Graham and the rest of the family. His outbursts would raise fear in his younger brothers. I felt like I was walking on eggshells in my own home, hoping not to upset Graham. Michael would say, "He knows what he's doing. He's taking advantage of us." I would then reply, "I don't think he understands everything. I think his Asperger syndrome is a disability to him, and we need to be more understanding." The truth was that neither of us knew for sure. Looking back, I think we were both right. However, we could never discern the real reasons for his behavior, so we rarely agreed on the needed response.

Now in eighth grade, Graham finally convinced me to quit fighting him on the medication. He stopped taking his ADHD medication, and I was pleasantly surprised to see a change in his behavior. He became less combative, but now he began earning bad grades and was in danger of failing. It seemed to always be something. One day, I received a call from the school asking me if I knew Graham had several one-hundred-dollar bills. "Are they real?" was my first question. Yes, they were real, and he was handing them out to students at school. I had no idea where Graham would get his hands on several hundred-dollar bills. I did, however, believe I knew why he would hand them out. He handed them out for the same reason he had handed out his medication last year. He wanted to make friends. He wanted people to like him.

Shortly after this phone call, our friend Ray called to ask if we had found his wallet. He hadn't seen it since his family had come over for dinner at our house the night before. Oh my, the pieces began to fall into place. "Ray, did you have any money in your wallet?" I asked as if I didn't know the answer. For some reason, Ray had $1,300 in his wallet, all in one-hundred-dollar bills. We confronted Graham as soon as he came home from school. He said he didn't know whose wallet it was and he just wanted to be a nice guy at school. We managed to recover some of the money. Graham worked off the remainder. Thank God Ray was extremely understanding.

As Christmas approached, I struggled with how we could help Graham. He was now off the medication he hated. The new doctor and therapist were good, but Graham continued to struggle. Graham was not happy, and he was asking to attend a different school. We prayed for God's intervention and clear guidance. We prayed for an answer. I knew we had a rebellious teenager on our hands. I also knew lots of Graham's struggle was because of the Asperger syndrome. We were trying everything we knew to try. Now he wanted another school. I wanted another school too, but where? I was convinced it had to be a school that was well versed in Asperger syndrome.

Graham had attended a summer camp in North Carolina a few years earlier that was for children with autism or AS. I called the camp to explain our dilemma, hoping for some wonderful words of advice. I remember saying, "If only there was a school that catered to Graham's AS." This is when they informed me that starting in January, the camp was opening the only school of its kind in the United States. It was a high school for kids with Asperger syndrome. I had to pinch myself. This was too good to be true. We started with the application immediately. Graham had been asking to go to a different school, and we were looking for someone to understand our child in ways only those who understood autism and AS could. Another piece of the pie just came into view. Would this be the final piece to complete the pie for Graham? Our hopes were high.

Graham started his new school a couple of months later in January. They agreed to complete eighth grade with him. I had high hopes that Graham would be able to excel at this special school. When they studied science, they were hands-on with all experiments. That was right up Graham's alley. When they studied history, they actually traveled to the places they were learning about. They had plans to visit Washington, DC, as well as one of the oldest cities in Florida. They would keep him busy with things he enjoyed and excelled in. On top of it all, they were specialists in Asperger syndrome. We thought this might be just what Graham needed. We enrolled Graham for the spring semester. I had visions of him loving

45

this school and attending all the way through high school. Now we could quit walking on eggshells at home. Michael and I drove Graham to North Carolina shortly after the new year. It was a small school of about ten kids. The staff was great. Graham seemed to quickly warm up to the idea of us leaving and him staying in a "boarding school" away from home.

The first month went well. But as they began traveling, Graham began to get frustrated with the staff and the other students. What I didn't count on was the fact that Graham was the highest-functioning student there. One of the rules was that if everyone can't participate, then no one does it. This was inhibiting and frustrating for Graham. We began getting calls that he was running away. The police were called on more than one occasion to help find him in the woods. I was afraid he would try to hitchhike home and be picked up by a pedophile or other predator. Thankfully, this never happened. When upset, he would always take off alone into the woods and camp out by himself. The last straw for the school happened while on a field trip. Graham got frustrated and tried to exit the van while traveling down the highway. He was back to his old tricks. That's when the school said that since they could no longer guarantee Graham's safety, they had to send him home.

This felt like a tragedy to us. What now? Graham would come home a failure. We were out of options. Thank goodness the school had a suggestion for us. They told us about a wilderness camp close to the school in North Carolina, which they recommended. The camp wasn't for criminals, just teens who were becoming rebellious. They hiked and camped with the kids for weeks, teaching them respect and teamwork. This was our only choice, and Michael and I agreed that Graham would enjoy the nonstop camping. The school even transported Graham to the camp. He stayed with them for six weeks, hiking, camping, and learning. He loved it and did so well. He would have stayed there much longer if we could have afforded it.

After six weeks, Michael and I went to pick Graham up. They performed a graduation ceremony for him. Each graduate was responsible for providing for their parents' stay at the campsite. Graham made a makeshift tent for us to sleep in that night. He filtered the river water for us to have clean drinking water. He even educated us on how to be safe from bears. The group encouraged and built Graham up as a leader. I was very proud of him. He came home a different young man. Our family realized we had to be different too. Via the telephone, Michael and I completed family counseling with the wilderness camp in order to prepare for Graham's return. Before bringing Graham home, we sat down with the three younger boys and discussed how we wanted to be a different family for Graham. Just as Graham had changed, we as a family needed to make some changes in order to help him have a better life.

The summer was very pleasant. We had a very organized summer schedule for Graham's comfort. As a homebuilder with his own business, Michael was able to take Graham with him three days a week. One day a week was a family excursion day. Sunday was reserved for church and time with Graham's mentor. The other two days were free days for Graham to do as he pleased. We were finally in such a good place with Graham. The entire family seemed to settle in to this new way of family life. Now we would continue to build on this newfound peace and grow from here.

Graham wanted to go back to his public school, so he entered high school that fall. Fortunately, the school in North Carolina did work with us over the summer, and Graham completed his eighth grade year. In order to go to public school, we had the agreement that if he didn't pass everything, we would look for an alternative school. Unfortunately, he didn't pass everything, so I found a charter school in the next town, and Graham started that January. Graham fit in well there. The teachers and administration encouraged creativity, and they were very flexible with the students. Graham made friends, and I once again hoped we had found our fit that would see him through graduation. All the different schools, mentors, therapists, doctors, and medications made the pie look like it might finally be complete.

However, as spring break approached, Graham and the family had slipped back into some of our old coping ways. He was the disgruntled teen, and we slipped back into anger and looking for the eggshells so as not to walk on them. But we had planned a spring break vacation. Hopefully this would be a time of fun and "reset" for our family. The whole family looked forward to going on this vacation together.

Boys (left to right) Blake, Jake, Graham, Titus

CHAPTER 4

A Vacation to Remember

Our family loves vacations. Michael and I said from the beginning of our marriage that we wanted to make family vacations
a priority. We believed this dedicated, secluded time away with
just the family unit could build lasting relationships and many
fond memories. Building memories became one of our top
goals as a family. When at all financially possible, we managed
to keep our vacations a priority. It is still fun to hear our sons
share their vacation stories. Trips to the beach were our most
frequent choice. This is where my boys first saw the ocean, went
on a crab hunt, built a sand castle, and learned to ride the waves
on a boogie board. The trip to Washington, DC, is remembered
as being the place where we saw money being made. Visiting
Georgia was a favorite for its river rafting down the frothy, wild
rapids. Of course, the trip to Colorado for skiing conjures up

different memories from each of the boys about the sparkling snow, majestic mountains, and learning to ski for the first time. And our vacation to Disney World was a blast, except, of course, when Graham decided to open the car door and try to get out while traveling down the freeway.

Unfortunately, not all the memories are good memories. The trip to Branson, Missouri, has to be my most memorable vacation, although it was not the most enjoyable. Graham was fifteen years old. He was not happy about being with the family, and he let us know it every chance he got. Basically, Graham was the typical disgruntled teenager times two. While visiting Branson, we did manage to enjoy going to a fascinating well-known magic show. We went on a hiking trip in an expansive wooded area where we also went cave exploring. As you can imagine, the muddy spelunking adventure was great fun for four young boys. The muddier we were, the better. We also enjoyed a rustic log cabin located right in the middle of the quiet pines.

One night, I was cooking a steak dinner while Michael was in the common area on the Internet. Graham was watching television, and the other boys were outside playing. Everyone but Graham was late getting back for dinner, so I made myself a plate and told Graham if he wanted dinner to come get it. As I took my plate and utensils to the couch, I asked Graham to move over so I could sit. He did a little shake (as if to move) but didn't move at all. I remember being so fed up with his disrespect that I wasn't going to ask nicely again. I happened to have a steak knife in my hand. Graham was leaning over on his left side, so I took the invitation and proceeded to poke him on his bottom with the knife and say, "Move." As I did, he jumped and slung his hand back to push the poke away. His hand hit the knife and slightly broke the skin. He yelled that I had stabbed him. Appalled by his statement, I said, "Oh my goodness, Graham, I didn't stab you. I just poked you to say move." With that, Graham ran to his dad to tell the story and get support against me. Michael must have been walking back to the cabin at the same time because they walked in together about ten minutes later. Michael, of course, took my side and told Graham that he should have moved. This made Graham all the more insistent that he had been wronged and we needed to acknowledge such abuse.

Now, I did recognize that the poking with the steak knife was not the action I should have taken, but it was on his bottom, and I certainly didn't mean for him to hit back and make a mark on his hand. However, Graham was screaming out to be heard. As Graham grew visibly angrier and Michael exhibited a nonchalant attitude toward him, I knew I needed to intervene. Graham needed us to see him as important enough to acknowledge his feelings. So I did just that. Graham was standing by the cabin's front door with his hand on the knob, ready to leave. Michael was sitting at the kitchen table, eating dinner and giving eye contact only to his food, tired of all the drama. The intensity of the situation was growing thick. As I sat on the couch in that tiny room, I remember looking Graham in the eyes and saying, "Graham, I am very sorry for poking you with the knife. I never intended to hurt you. Would you please forgive me?" Now, this is something we had learned to do with our children years earlier. I apologized often to each one of them and always followed up with the question, "Will you please forgive me?" We desired for our kids to learn compassion and forgiveness, and of course, it should start with us. This incident was no exception. I would apologize. He would forgive me, and we would move on. Only that did not happen this time.

Immediately after I apologized, Graham reluctantly said, "Okay." He let go of the doorknob and moved to sit down. He had taken two steps toward the couch when Michael said, "It wasn't a big deal. You should just have obeyed her." No sooner were these words out of my husband's mouth than Graham got a look of determination on his face, quickly turned, and marched out of the house. I was not happy with Michael, and we argued for a bit about how we handled the situation. I thought we needed to acknowledge Graham's feelings and give him some time to think and cool off. Michael felt we were letting him get away with being manipulative again, so he didn't want to admit any wrongdoing. I didn't know where Graham had gone, but I hoped he would cool off quickly and come home. Within two hours, Graham did come back to the cabin. What I didn't count on was him showing up with two police officers.

Michael was in the room when Graham walked through the door with two very serious officers in tow. I was at the back getting ready for bed when I heard Michael talking with another gentleman. My first thought was, *I hope Graham is all right.* As I walked from the back of the cabin, one very large officer stepped up to me and asked in a loud voice, "Did you pull a knife on this boy?" I was stunned.

Of course, I didn't "pull a knife" on my son. When I tried to explain, the police officer told me he had been abused as a boy by his mother too, and he would not allow this. He said he had no choice but to arrest me. I was absolutely stunned. Graham stood there with a sheepish look on his face as if to say, *I didn't want to have to do this, but I just had to do it.* My husband and I tried to explain our family dynamics, but it was like talking to a wall. Michael tried insisting with the officer, but he told him to stand down. They began to handcuff me with all four children in the room. I asked them to please let me walk to the patrol car for the sake of my younger children. One memory I never wanted my kids to have was of mom being arrested. I kissed Michael, Jake, Titus, and Blake good-bye. I told the kids I was fine and that I would see them tomorrow. The policemen, Graham, and I walked to the patrol car, where I was handcuffed before climbing into the backseat.

In case you've never been in the back of a patrol car, let me tell you, it is very tight seating, especially if you have your hands cuffed behind your back. I was in shock. I was extremely uncomfortable, and I was scared. I was in a strange state, sup-posedly on vacation, with my hands confined and a man who seemed to hate me as if I were his own abusive mother. As soon as I climbed into the car and the door closed behind me, I began to cry uncontrollably. As the officer closed the door, he must have started to soften because I heard him tell my son that if that were his mom, he would feel bad. Graham just said, "She shouldn't have pulled a knife on me." I cried harder.

The officers had arrived in two different vehicles. When the first vehicle left long before we did, I was truly concerned for my own safety. I was with the officer who seemed to have already tried and convicted me of his own mother's crimes. My imagination went wild. This officer could stop along the way, in the dark, and I was totally defenseless. We drove in silence, except for my whimpering. I was immensely relieved to arrive at the jail. I was given gray scrubs to wear. They took my clothes. They took my picture and my fingerprints. It was the middle of the night, so I was led to a dark cell and locked up. I later learned the woman I shared a cell with had been charged with possession of methamphetamines. She was a rough character, and I was out of my league to say the least.

When I entered, she spoke to me in the dark, saying I could have the top bunk. She was sleeping on the bottom. I climbed up, hoping she would stay down there. She introduced herself as Brenda. I'll never forget her first question. The question I never thought I would hear. I certainly never wanted to hear it. "So what are you in for?" I explained as quickly as I could. I really wasn't in the mood for a conversation. However, I was less in the mood for making a locked-up criminal mad at me. She took my side and said she couldn't believe my son would do such a thing to me. I, to be fair, took her side when she explained that the drugs she was caught with didn't belong to her. Everyone in jail is innocent, you know. Eventually she quit talking and went to sleep.

I think I might have fallen asleep for an hour or two. Most of the night, I lay awake and cried. I absolutely couldn't believe this. I was stupid and let my emotions move me to poking Graham, and he had me arrested. I had a master's degree in social work and was now being charged with child abuse with a deadly weapon. Would I be convicted and spend time in jail? And even if I was released, how would I ever get a job in the field of social work again? This was sure to affect the rest of my children. Wouldn't Social Services have to open a case for all my children now to determine if I was a fit mom for them? I was afraid of being convicted and going to jail. I was afraid of never getting a job in my field again. I was afraid of losing my children. I was also physically afraid of this lady with whom I was sharing a locked cell. With all those concerns, my biggest fear by far was how would I ever forgive Graham for doing this. He wanted to prove to his father that this was a big deal and that someone would believe him and take his side. Now I sat in jail and cried for my future and for the seemingly lost relationship with my son.

I lay awake in the top bunk of that dark cell, and I talked with God. I remember begging Him to take this away. I asked Him to forgive me for not being a good mom. I asked Him to help Graham. Then I asked Him to get even with Graham. I told Him I was so mad and was afraid I would never forgive Graham. I knew forgiveness was a big deal. According to Matthew chapter 6, if I couldn't forgive my son, God would not forgive me of my wrongdoing. No matter the legal outcome of this situation, I was deathly afraid of losing my relationship with Graham. He had gone too far, and now I would never forgive him. The consequences of that unforgiveness would surely spread throughout the family relationships. How would we even be a family again if I was unable to forgive? I was in a spiritual battle for my family that night. It all hinged on my forgiving Graham. I knew it was right to forgive, but I didn't want to forgive. Then I wanted to forgive, but I didn't feel like forgiving. Fear gripped me all night. I felt like the devil himself was crouching around the corner, ready to pounce on me, on my husband, on Graham, on my other children. It was a terrible tug-of-war. I knew forgiving was a command of God; therefore, it was a choice I could make, whether I *felt* like it or not. So I began a back and forth for hours. "God, I choose to forgive him...I'm so mad at him and want nothing to do with him again...God, I choose to forgive him...Please help me feel like forgiving him...I don't forgive him...He's so ungrateful...I think I hate him...God, I choose to forgive him." It was a very long night.

By the time morning had arrived, I knew I had chosen to forgive Graham. I can't explain how, except to say that forgiveness is a supernatural act. God Himself allows us to experience the choice of forgiveness, but we have to make that decision. I think it is a trust in God Himself more than anything. If God wanted me to make this decision, then I needed to trust that it was for the best and He would take care of my feelings for and relationship with Graham. I was determined to walk in that forgiveness even though I was still very angry with him. Graham was my son, and my God would enable me to do the right thing. God would give me the grace to do what He had instructed me to do. I had to trust in God. I couldn't trust that Graham would ever be sorry for this. I couldn't trust myself to forgive and really put this behind me. I didn't know how to do it. I knew I really couldn't do it on my own by mere self-will. *But* I knew my God could do this in me. I entrusted myself to Him.

They woke us up at 4:00 a.m. or 5:00 a.m. to receive breakfast. Needless to say, I did not eat. I gained some points with Brenda when I gave her my oatmeal and toast. After breakfast was the time we were to clean our cells. Brenda told me it was my turn to clean the toilet. I totally agreed with her and cleaned whatever she told me to clean. Then everyone went back to sleep. The whole experience seems surreal to me now. I could not go back to sleep. I proceeded to lie on my bunk and talk with God, solidifying my forgiveness decision. To my great relief, my cellmate had a court date that morning and left the cell at 9:00 a.m. I remained in the cell hoping that no one else would wander in to be my friend. I had no interest in being friendly. I was physically, emotionally, and spiritually exhausted. I was still afraid of how this situation would turn out. I thought of Michael and the boys. I was praying that Michael had been calm. I was praying that he and Graham had not had any altercation during the evening hours. Mostly, I was praying that Michael was out the door early that morning and getting me out of this jail.

Lunch came at 11:00 a.m. I wasn't hungry then either but was forced to come to the common area. Brenda was still gone, so I gave my lunch tray to the first woman who asked. When I was finally allowed to go back to my cell, I was praying I wouldn't have to stay another night here. It was around 1:00 p.m. when they told me to bring my bedding down because I was being released. Michael had managed to speak with the district attorney who miraculously understood the situation and dropped all charges. That was a very difficult afternoon. I was determined to continue our vacation as if this had not occurred. I wanted the boys to have good memories even if I had one really bad one. It was difficult for me to even look at Graham. I had chosen to forgive him, but my feelings did not easily follow. I think I had to choose to forgive him every few minutes that first day.

The fact that I had an arrest record haunted me for some time, but I was assured it would not be an issue. The next year, when I applied for a job with the Census Bureau, they told me I had a mark on my record and would have to complete more paperwork. I was certain it was this incident that was marking my record. I just dropped the application for fear that I would be dragged back into anger over the situation again.

Choosing forgiveness was not over once I was released. I continued to choose forgiveness every time I thought of that night. Over time, God gave me an overwhelming love for my son, but I had to choose forgiveness over and over again, maybe a thousand times. My feelings of forgiveness finally did follow. I am so grateful to God because I know it is only by His grace that I made the decision to forgive. And it is God's miracle that the feelings did follow. I never expected to hear an apology from Graham, although I longed for one. The young man who could only see black and white believed he was completely justified in calling the police and having me arrested. I'm sure in his mind, he needed to get his point across to us, and whatever it took to do that was the right thing to do. I forgave Graham and put the whole thing behind us. I didn't bring it back up to him, nor did he speak of it for many years.

CHAPTER 5

A Descending Journey

In the fall of 2008, Graham was sixteen years old, and his brother Jake was turning fifteen. They both landed jobs at the local McDonald's, and although he enjoyed the charter school, Graham continued to struggle in his studies. Over the next year, Graham failed to pass all of his classes again. However, he did have friends and seemed to be studying a little. He even had his first long-term girlfriend. We decided to keep Graham in the charter school, mainly because we had exhausted all other options. This school was full of creative and what I call *off-the-grid* people. In some ways, I found this refreshing and good for Graham, who was so "off-the-grid" himself. However, not everything was as it seemed.

Little did I know that Graham was just starting a long, slow descending journey. Our parenting struggles were about to get harder, and our faith was about to be tested like never before. During his tenth grade year, we made a very disturbing discovery. Graham was participating in a ritual where he would cut himself with a knife or razor blade to obtain emotional relief. The common term is *cutting*. Although I had heard of cutting, I was not very familiar with it. Apparently, some people cut themselves as a self-harming method of coping. It is a way to be distracted from your life and release your emotional pain. This type of release is difficult to understand or explain. But this is a simplistic explanation that helped me: when one has internal pain and anxiety building, for a moment, when he/she cuts themselves, their physical body hurts just like their internal self does; in that moment, they feel a temporary release and relief. I am convinced it is just another tool our enemy, the devil, uses to keep them from seeking out the real and permanent solution—Jesus Christ. This distraction and release does work for them, but only temporarily. The problem becomes increasingly serious, however, because the longer one engages in this behavior, the deeper the cut required for any type of release. In other words, the longer someone uses this method for relief, the more dangerous the action becomes.

When I first saw Graham's arms, I was horrified. He must have been cutting awhile before we noticed because he had several cuts from his wrist to his elbow. Some cuts were fresh, and some appeared to be scars. Some were long and wide while others were small in size. He usually wore long sleeves, which didn't seem odd to me since Graham had odd sensitivities to clothing, so he often dressed differently. This particular day, his sleeve accidently lifted as we were discussing something, and I saw the cuts on his forearm. Terrified, I insisted he tell me what had happened. He didn't say much. I'm sure he was overwhelmed by my strong reaction and didn't know how to explain the violent ritual he was involved in on a consistent basis. I saw that my reaction was inhibiting his openness with us, so I talked myself down and relaxed a little for his sake. Michael and I talked with him about his worth and our availability to help him, but Graham still did not engage in the conversation.

As I researched this act of cutting, I discovered it was usually done because of extreme anxiety. This was no surprise as Graham had suffered from anxiety for several years now. We informed his therapist and discussed it with his doctor. The best they could do for him was talk therapy and a prescription for a stronger antianxiety medication. We talked with his church mentor, David, so he could speak with Graham on that personal buddy level as well. We prayed and loved on Graham as best we knew how in order to steer him away from this destructive act. His cutting didn't completely stop, but we believed he engaged in the ritual less and less. We felt we were going in the right direction.

Within a few months, we were moving into a new house. As we packed, we found many empty cough syrup bottles hidden around the house. Again, I did my research and discovered that common over-the-counter cough syrup has an ingredient called DXM, which teens frequently use to obtain a high called *dexing*. The many empty cough syrup bottles we found told us that Graham had found yet another way to abuse drugs. We had hoped the antianxiety medication and therapy would curb his need to escape reality, but our hopes were once again dashed. To add to our fear and disappointment, it was also around this time that we discovered Graham was continuing to huff or inhale chemicals. He inhaled propane from the grill tanks or any random spray can that happened to be available. We tried to explain to him that these chemicals would do irreparable damage to his brain cells. This information alone did not change Graham's need for relief and escape. He continued to inhale propane and any aerosol with an intoxicating chemical he found. We locked up every can, tank, and prescription bottle we could find. Not only was Graham inhaling, he continued drinking cough syrup. It also became clear that he was smoking marijuana. Apparently, drugs were commonplace at his charter school. This was how Graham fit in at school and how he coped with his anxiety.

One of the most disturbing problems for the whole family was Graham's inability to sleep. I'm sure it was his lack of sleep that drove him to abuse the cough syrup and marijuana. Most nights, he was awake watching TV or working on his computer projects. This lack of sleep added to his anxiety level to such an extent that sometimes he would burst into our room in the middle of the night, flip the light on, and begin pacing around, crying. He was in a full-blown panic attack. He begged us for help. We prayed over him and with him. We encouraged him to breathe deeply to calm down. We felt absolutely helpless. Needless to say, we received less sleep as well.

Frantic to find help, we sought advice from the school, local counseling centers, and our pastor. This is when a friend from church talked with us about a drug rehabilitation program he had gone through in Portland, Oregon. It was a Christian center and highly recommended by our friend. The most amazing thing was that the program was free. The economy had recently taken a downturn, and our business had been a victim, so this was a true Godsend. After many phone calls on my part and the intervention of our friend, Graham was accepted into the program. Graham did not want to leave his girlfriend, but he reluctantly agreed to go after she encouraged him.

Shortly after he turned seventeen years old, Graham traveled to Portland, Oregon, and entered the rehabilitation program. Again, our hopes were high. Maybe this piece of the pie would make it complete. The first few weeks, we couldn't speak with our son. They wanted to get his complete attention. It was a program that included God and His Word. God's promises were spoken over him, and he was encouraged to follow after Jesus. After the isolation time, we talked with Graham every week. He was doing well, although he was still not allowed to have phone conversations with his girlfriend. He hadn't shared any big revelation or turnaround, but there was lots of time. Honestly, the time without Graham at home was restful. I did feel somewhat guilty about feeling relief, but I think it was a natural and needed rest after so many years of challenges. Knowing that Graham was in good hands, we relaxed a bit and enjoyed our other three boys.

To be successful, the program called for eight months of residential treatment. However, true to form, after three months, Graham wanted to leave. Graham was told by the program that he would be able to speak with his girlfriend as well as his family over the phone. When this promise was not kept, it was all he could think about. He demanded they comply with their promise. But they did not. The treatment became more personal and demanded more out of him, but Graham couldn't go deeper with them because his mind was on their broken promise. He called home, begging to leave the program. When we told him he needed to stay and get well, Graham began working on a plan to get kicked out. He conjured up a plan, pulling from his past experience at the school in North Carolina. We received a call from the administration exactly three months after he had arrived at the center. They informed us that Graham had intentionally walked in front of oncoming traffic. They were shocked at his behavior and afraid of the possibility he would be hurt. Then I heard familiar words, "We have no choice but to send him home." They could no longer guarantee his safety, so they could no longer have him in the program. Disappointment once again flooded my heart. When will this ever end? How will we deal with Graham's addictions when he returns home?

I fell on my bed in tears. I cried out to God in complete surrender. "I don't know what to do! I'm apparently not good at being Graham's mom. I want Graham to be free. I want him to enjoy life. I want to enjoy him. I've got to believe You want this too. *Please*, don't just help me with Graham. *You* have to do this. *I* can't do this. I get out of the way. You do what he needs. It's got to be You." I have never heard God speak audibly, but I did hear Him speak loud and clear to my heart at that moment. He said, "Graham is going to get it." It was so real that I sat straight up in bed and said, "What?" God said it again, "Graham is going to get it." I chose to believe that day that my God was going to get hold of Graham in one way or another. God was pursuing Graham. I still wasn't sure what I needed to do, but I would keep on walking, stumbling, and getting back up. God had told me Graham was going to "get it," and I was going to believe Him.

Graham was on his way home, and we were at a loss as to how to proceed with him. We sent money for Graham to take a bus home from Portland, Oregon, to Austin, Texas. I'm sure that was a very long ride for him. He probably needed that long ride to consider all he had done and what future was ahead of him at home. Michael and I certainly needed that time to consider how we were to navigate this part of the journey. We had told Graham, when he was asking to come home, that he wasn't allowed to come back home without completing the program. He didn't know what to expect from us now. We sure didn't know what to expect from him. He looked very apprehensive when I picked him up from the bus stop. I hugged him hello. Graham had been on a bus for three days, and he smelled like it. The tension in the car was so thick it could have been cut with a knife. Neither of us wanted to tackle the conversation of, *What now?* I just told him he needed to get rested up over the next couple of days; then the three of us would sit down to discuss the future.

We did not enroll him again in the charter school or the public school. He was so far behind in his studies and the charter school was where he got deeper into drug usage, so we agreed Graham needed to take the GED tests. Graham assured us that he had been clean from drugs for the last three months, and he wanted to stay that way for his girlfriend. It became clear to me that he was unable to focus on recovery because all he ever thought about was the girlfriend. We made it clear to Graham that he needed to obtain his GED and get a job. He was almost eighteen years old and would need to move out of our home if he continued to disrespect us and cause chaos. We told him we would always be his parents, and we would always love him. We specifically said to him, "We want you to stay with us as long as you need in order to become a mature, healthy person, but you have to treat yourself and your family with respect." It seemed that all Graham ever wanted to do was leave our home. Now this wish might come true very soon if he couldn't stick with our agreement. Unfortunately, we did not feel as if we had the time to instill the proper preparation he needed to live on his own. Our plans for Graham and his life were not working out at all as we had thought they would.

Graham seemed to receive all we had to say about obtaining his GED, getting a job, and respecting our family. Obtaining his GED came fairly easy for him. Graham was very intelligent. He had always been an avid reader. Tests were not hard for him, so when he took the four GED tests, he passed them all the first time and with very high scores. However, Graham struggled with his job search. He didn't make a good first impression since he had trouble looking people in the eye, shaking hands, and feeling confident of himself. He had no job prospects, no school to attend, and his anxiety began to rise.

It was exactly four months after he returned home that Graham's girlfriend broke up with him. As with most teen romances, this one too lost its flame. It was no one's fault. It was just a normal high school interest fizzled out. At least that's how she felt. Graham, however, had given his whole heart and was counting on this relationship to save him from his destructive feelings and behaviors. He quickly found out that he could not count on a girlfriend to save him. Graham went into immediate depression. I woke up one morning to find one bottle of his medications empty. He admitted that he had taken them the day before in an attempt to take his life. Thank God this attempt did not succeed. As I talked with him, I knew I was getting nowhere. Michael and I were afraid that he would attempt suicide again and this time be successful. My mind began to play out the scenario of waking one morning to find Graham lifeless in his bed.

Graham refused to go with me to the hospital for a mental health evaluation. I was afraid for my son's life and needed a plan quickly. I called his past probation officer, who suggested that since he was still a minor, I could call and report to the police that he had been using drugs in our home. Once he was arrested, he could be evaluated. That was the drastic yet loving action we took. That afternoon, the probation officer and a police officer arrived at our house, surprising Graham and arresting him for drug use. He went kicking and screaming. I'll never forget how he screamed and cursed at me all the way to the police car. He yelled that I would never see him again. He yelled that I was the reason now that he would die. It's almost unbearable for me, even to this day, to recall and write down his words. I have never wanted anything more than life and love for my son Graham. Now he hated me, black and white. No gray area for grace or forgiveness.

His anxiety and depression had taken over his life. We did the best we knew how. We felt we had tried everything. Doctors, medications, therapists, special schools, rehabilitation—they all fell short of seeing Graham rise above his challenges. Why had God allowed such heartache for Graham and for us as his parents? We were all experiencing heartache. But I felt especially helpless when I thought of how much pain Graham must be experiencing. He must be so lonely, so anxious, so depressed. How would we ever help him? How would he ever be whole? God needed to come in and do a work here. And Graham needed to make better decisions.

Part of me wanted to go with Graham to make sure they took good care of him. Part of me knew I needed a break and some time. I needed to trust that God had this. I really couldn't trust the jail personnel, but I had to trust that God loved Graham more than even I did. My God had told me He would pursue Graham and that Graham would "get it." But when was he going to get it? I was hanging on by a thread. My fears of the jail personnel were realized when I found out that they left Graham in a jail cell alone with some personal items they should have removed. They also did not give him constant supervision. Graham was so angry he choked himself with his shoestrings. They found him fainted on the floor of his cell. This incident is what they used to make an involuntary commitment to the state mental hospital.

I quickly discovered this mental hospital was not the place for Graham to receive true help. In an attempt to calm Graham down, the hospital gave him such a high dose of medication that he was put into a zombie state. Our first visit consisted of watching Graham sit on the couch and drool as he attempted to speak with us. After several days, he began seeing a counselor and a psychiatrist. The counselor took a backseat to the psychiatrist, whose sole job was to discover the right medication for Graham. Graham left the hospital three weeks later with stronger antianxiety medications and medications to handle the bad side effects of the stronger antianxiety medications. I knew deep in my heart that medicating the symptoms was only a Band-Aid. I continued taking one step at a time. I didn't know how to help Graham. He was tangled up in anger, depression, and anxiety. I felt totally helpless. We continued to pray and talk openly about Graham's situation with others, hoping real help would surface and God's promise of "Graham getting it" would be realized.

Graham returned home three weeks after he was admitted to the hospital, and the family arguments began again. He was highly annoyed by his younger eleven-year-old brother, and he began threatening him. He would scream at him, saying he was going to hurt him. Blake tried to stay clear of Graham for fear that he would make good on his threats. Michael and I feared for Blake's safety as well. We knew it was a very good possibility that Graham could lose his temper and justify any violent action he took toward defenseless eleven-year-old Blake. We did our best to never allow the two of them to be home alone. The stress was felt by everyone in the household. There was no peace or laughter. We were back to walking on very delicate eggshells. Something had to break soon.

The break became reality one day as I drove home from work to find three police cars in the driveway. This was not an everyday occurrence, but it wasn't a big surprise either. As I drove up toward the house, my jaw dropped to see blood on the carport. My mind didn't have time to consider all the horrible possibilities before a policeman greeted me at my car. He informed me that my son Graham had been arrested for striking his father in the head with a rock. Just then, Michael walked out of the house with the top of his head bleeding profusely. He and Graham had gotten into a heated argument. Michael explained that this argument over Graham's lack of respect for the family escalated into a fight. Graham ran outside, and Michael followed him. Graham then picked up a rock from the yard and threw it toward his dad. Michael ducked, but the rock did hit him on the top of his head. Tired of the confrontations and afraid of Graham's next action, Michael told Blake to call 911.

When the police arrived, they didn't need Dad to press charges. They saw the result of the physical assault and arrested Graham on the spot. We were not willing to press charges. If Graham was going to get into serious trouble, it had to be of his own accord without our involvement. I wanted Graham to see us as the ones who helped rescue him from trouble, not as a part of that trouble. If we were anywhere in the vicinity, he usually found a way to blame us. The police knew we would be unwilling to act legally, so in an attempt to protect our family, the police filed a restraining order against Graham. The order stated that Graham couldn't come near his dad for a period of six months. I took Michael to the nearest hospital, where he received eight staples in his head. Graham went to the county jail to await a court hearing. Although he was seventeen years old, he would be treated as an adult and incarcerated in the county jail.

CHAPTER 6

Turning of Age

I visited Graham in the county jail. Now that he was being treated as an adult, the jail experience was totally different. We were only able to visit through a glass window and talk via a telephone. The narrow room consisted of a long wall of windows with ten steel stools divided evenly in front of the window. Each sitting area had a small divider between it. I filed in with several other families to find Graham sitting at one of the seats on the other side of the glass. I sat, and he dialed the phone, which then rang my phone, in order for us to have a conversation. Graham was in a gray jumpsuit. The conversations were difficult since it was hard to hear through the static on the phone, not to mention the lack of privacy. Mostly, he justified his actions with Michael. Graham told me he was afraid when Michael walked toward him, so he grabbed a rock and threw it. I do not believe Graham intended the rock to hurt his dad, just as I'm sure Michael was not coming toward Graham with any ill intent. Fear, anger, and spontaneous reactions were taking our family deeper into a crevasse I wasn't sure we could climb out of anytime soon. I couldn't stand the fact that a domestic incident put Graham in jail. Graham's jail bond was more than we could afford at the time. However, even if we could have easily afforded it, we didn't know where he would go since he wasn't allowed home. Because of the restraining order, Graham stayed incarcerated, and I visited him weekly, waiting for the court date.

We kept David, Graham's mentor, well informed of everything going on with Graham. We always called David when conversations with Graham would turn ugly or when Graham was making harmful decisions. There were times he acted as our sounding board as well. David also never held back when Michael and I needed to hear words of correction. Many times over the years, it was David's intervention that God used to help bring peace back to our home. Graham and David were very close, and Graham considered David to be a trusted and close friend. We naturally called David about the altercation between Michael and Graham and about Graham's arrest. After a few weeks, David called me. "Lore, with your permission, I'd like to bail Graham out of jail. But he has to have a place to go." Graham legally couldn't come home. David traveled weekly for his job, so living in his home wasn't an option. I did want Graham free. I hated the thought of him in jail. The only person we could think to ask was Michael's mother, Graham's grandma. Grandma lived a short hour's drive from us in Round Rock, Texas. Graham had always been sweet and thoughtful of his grandma when he was younger. She loved Graham and felt they had a special relationship. Michael and I decided to ask Grandma to consider having Graham live with her till this restraining order passed. Hopefully by then, we would have more answers. For now, we lived day by day.

When Michael called to ask if she would consider having Graham come live with her for a while, she agreed without hesitation. We all hoped the change of scenery and being out from under Mom and Dad would help. David bailed Graham out, and I picked Graham up to deliver him to his grandma's house. He settled in with Grandma, helped her around the house, and started looking for a job. I saw him every other week, taking him to doctor and court appointments. The court gave Graham a six-month probation sentence for assaulting his father. I drove to pick him up every two weeks for probation appointments. The drive to Grandma's was an hour, then an hour back to probation, then an hour back to Grandma's, then an hour back home. I hoped Graham would appreciate me. I hoped the time we spent together in the car would be fruitful in forming a better relationship. But Graham was more discouraged than ever, and he took it out on me. If he talked at all, he argued with me. Arguments covered everything from life with Grandma to what we would eat for lunch. It's sad to say, but I was grateful he was not at home. At least I only had to deal with his attitude twice a month.

Graham unfortunately continued his unemployment streak. After several months, the stress took its toll on him, and his anxiety rose. I didn't realize how bad things were getting until Grandma called one day. "Lore, something is really wrong with Graham. He is laughing one minute and in tears the next." I thought he was probably abusing drugs again and that he might have some other mental issues. I asked Graham if he wanted me to find a psychiatrist near him. When he agreed, I made an appointment with a trusted psychiatrist. The only problem was the appointment wasn't for two weeks. Our family was preparing for a road trip to visit my family in Kentucky. Graham said he would like to go with us. Although we were concerned about vacationing with Graham again, Michael and I agreed it was necessary to begin mending the family. We contacted his probation officer, and Graham was granted permission to travel out of state. While we waited for the psychiatrist appointment, I thought it would be good to get Graham away from everything and have a fun visit with the family. He would enjoy seeing all of his cousins. It was our first opportunity to have Graham and Michael together again with the whole family unit. Hopefully, this would be a good trip to get away from day-to-day stress. This was the first vacation since the infamous Branson, Missouri, trip, so I was a little nervous. Michael and I jokingly agreed no steak dinners on this vacation.

The day before we were to leave for Kentucky, Grandma called me at noon. She had just discovered that Graham had left the house during the night. The police were at the door informing her that Graham had been arrested for breaking and entering. I asked to speak with the officer, and he explained to me that Graham had been picked up walking the streets at 5:00 a.m. They considered him suspicious because of the early hour and the fact that he was wearing a hoodie in the hot weather. When they stopped him, he was hiding a laptop under his sweatshirt and had a prescription bottle that was not his. Upon investigation, they discovered the owner of the prescription medication had her home burglarized earlier that night. The laptop was also missing from a business that had been broken into and burglarized. Graham was arrested and charged with breaking and entering and burglary. He was one month short of his eighteenth birthday, so he was charged as an adult.

We were unable to visit or even contact Graham for about a week. When I called the jail for information, I found out there was a lot of red tape involved in visitation. Graham had to complete a visitation list before we were allowed to visit. The main problem is the fact that no one gave Graham instructions. He was left to discover all information on his own. We were waiting for him to prepare the way for us to visit, and he was in the dark as to what to do. I made several calls and complaints and sent up lots of prayers. Finally, Graham called us. I was able to instruct him on the visitation list, and within a couple of more weeks, that was complete for us to schedule a time to see Graham.

Before we were able to visit Graham in person, he was appointed an attorney. I found out through his attorney that Graham had been given a mental health evaluation in jail. The doctor diagnosed him with bipolar disorder and in need of more medication. It was very difficult seeing my son behind a glass in an orange jumpsuit, which denotes mental illness. All my dreams for my firstborn seemed to be sailing away. Graham had always been smart, active, and intense. We prayed for him, with him, took him to church every Sunday, and guided him toward Jesus as best we could. When Graham was seven years old, he wanted to pray and receive Christ into his life. Michael and I talked with Graham seriously about what Christ had done for us and how we needed Jesus in order to have a true connection with God. Graham appeared to understand and desired to say yes to Jesus. Afterward, he was very excited. The next morning, a neighborhood boy came over to play. Graham jumped up and down, performing the Asperger syndrome routine we later came to know as flapping. He told Phillip he was so happy that he had asked Jesus into his life, and now he wanted to know if Phillip wanted to do the same. What a joy to my heart to believe Graham was now a child of God. Somehow depression and anxiety had crept into our family and stolen Graham away. Now, almost eleven years later, I sat in a county jail, talking with my beloved son through a glass window as he faced a very serious criminal charge.

Between Graham and the police report, I managed to put the story of that unbelievable night together. That evening Graham was feeling overwhelmed and was unable to sleep. He was most likely experiencing one of his panic attacks. He found some of Grandma's sleeping pills and took a couple before leaving the house. I'm not sure if he had a destination in mind, but the sleeping aid he ingested has a reputation for allowing the person taking the drug to sleepwalk. He left in the middle of the night and, for some reason, entered an elderly lady's home a few streets away. He said the door was unlocked. While she slept, Graham drank a Gatorade and watched television. Before leaving, he stole some sleeping pills from her bathroom. He then proceeded to enter the duplex next door to find a family watching television. Startled, they jumped up and threatened Graham with a gun. He ran out of the duplex and wandered the streets until he decided to break into a place of business. It was here Graham stole a laptop computer. Graham was arrested a few hours later and incarcerated in the toughest county in Texas.

A few weeks later, Graham turned eighteen years old in the county jail. We visited him often. Although the visitation in this county jail was also through a glass window, we were allowed private visits. Without ten other families and screaming children in the room, we could visit more comfortably. They added to Graham's medications because of the bipolar and anxiety diagnosis. I knew of this county's reputation for being very hard with offenders and issuing much longer sentences than other counties for the same crime. I could only hope that Graham's diagnosis of Asperger syndrome, anxiety disorder, and now bipolar disorder would stir the court's compassion as they realized the extent of his disabilities. I worked with the court-appointed attorney, getting her all the records of Graham's medical history. His crime was not a violent crime. He had mental issues, and this was his first offense outside the family charge. No one in the prosecuting attorney's office gave any weight to Graham's medical issues, his age, or his lack of violence. They came to court asking the judge to send Graham to the state prison for eight years. I was in total shock. I had never heard of a young man of eighteen years old being sent to prison for a nonviolent crime, especially when he has mental health issues.

Because it was his first offense, his court-appointed attorney managed to get Graham deferred adjudication. This meant Graham was sentenced to the eight years of prison, but he could serve his sentence out of prison and on probation. If he messed up even once, he would automatically go to prison for eight years. Graham had gotten arrested in the toughest county of Texas, notorious for harsh sentencing. They didn't care that he had been experiencing a bipolar episode or that he was only seventeen years old or that this was his first offense. Nothing was under my control. I remember shaking my head and thinking, *How in the world did this happen? How in the world will Graham manage the next eight years with the police watching his every move?*

Several months after his arrest, Graham was released on probation. His probation officer and his required classes were all in Grandma's town, so I took him back to Grandma's house. He now had even more medication, along with a psychiatrist and probation officer to visit every week. He now qualified for special services, which would help him obtain a job. The medication he was on did seem to help Graham with his anxiety. He left the jail determined to get a job and do well. He didn't want to end up in prison. My biggest fear was that I knew the chances of Graham staying completely out of trouble for eight whole years were slim to none.

CHAPTER 7

Holding On by a Thread

Graham returned to Grandma's home with renewed hope. We all had our hope renewed. The new medication seemed to help. Graham was calmer and was actually sleeping at night. He was more focused as well. He began to focus on educating himself about his medications. Graham had always loved research. His need for medications evoked a desire in him to understand the drugs and the purpose of each. Graham investigated all his symptoms, diagnoses, and medications. He became an expert in his own eyes. Graham began to request many different medications from his doctors as they attempted to discover exactly what medications would work best with him. He was busy educating himself on the different drugs available for the different diagnoses, meeting with his probation officer, attending the court-ordered classes, and looking for a job. When he wasn't quickly successful at obtaining a job, Graham decided to take some college courses at a nearby college. Michael and I helped him get enrolled and maneuver financial aid. He didn't have transportation, so Graham started all his classes online.

Almost a year after receiving his eight-year probation sentence, Graham seemed to be managing well. He was enrolled in school and keeping all of his required meetings for probation. However, Grandma was very displeased with him at home. Graham was not cleaning up after himself, he talked disrespectfully to her, and he still had not found a job. He insisted he was helping, and Grandma was being unreasonable. After a visit with him, I discovered he was not keeping up with his online classes either. I began to wonder if he had started abusing his medication again. Grandma wanted Graham to leave, and we were back in the old familiar place of no options.

It was carnival time in our little hometown, so I brought Graham home for the weekend. Grandma had done all she could to help Graham, but she was experiencing health problems and didn't want him to come back. Operating one day at a time, I brought Graham home and prayed that God would give us some clear direction. Friday night, we had a family dinner and welcomed Graham home. All the boys were happy about the carnival being in town and were looking forward to spending the weekend with their friends. Saturday morning, Michael and I both had to work. Graham was sleeping late, and the rest of the boys headed to the carnival. Graham did eventually rise and, I assume, made his way to the carnival. But unfortunately, he did not make it home that night. Convincing myself that he had connected with old friends and spent the night with them, I waited for his return. I only hoped that probation and the real threat of eight years in prison would keep him away from drugs and trouble. Slowly but surely, I was overwhelmed by suspicion. Sunday afternoon, there was no sign of Graham, so I decided to call the police station. If he wasn't there, then surely he would wander home by Monday. To my dismay, Graham had been arrested Saturday afternoon. At the time, I didn't know the whole story, but I did know he was now in grave danger of going to prison.

Graham was charged with breaking and entering at a neighbor's home as well as shoplifting from a local grocery store. When he finally woke up two days later in jail, he remembered very little of that weekend. He did remember feeling anxious and taking four sleeping pills Saturday morning. He then proceeded to walk to the carnival. I'm not sure why he thought he could still function with one sleeping pill, let alone four, but he did. After that, the next two days were a blur to him.

According to the police report, Graham walked to our neighbor's house and proceeded to break the glass of their sliding back door. The owner of the house was home. Standing in the house, he shouted at Graham to stop. The owner stated that Graham seemed "out of it." Graham didn't respond to the owner's shouts but suddenly saw him and ran away. The police were called, and the search for Graham began. They didn't have to search for long. An hour later, the local grocery store called in a shoplifting incident. It was Graham, and he matched the description of the attempted breaking and entering suspect. Once arrested, he slept for the better part of two days.

This was a different county than where he was on probation, so a different attorney was appointed to represent him. God's grace was on us as I am positive He handpicked Mr. Jones to be Graham's attorney. Mr. Jones took a special interest in Graham. He saw a young man with mental health issues. He didn't just do the minimum, which was what I'm sure he was being paid since he was court-appointed. Mr. Jones went out of his way to understand Graham by talking with us and by researching Asperger syndrome and bipolar disorder. He spoke with several mental health specialists and worked hard to keep Graham in his county. He knew if our county worked Graham through this recent charge quickly, he would be sent back to the harsh county immediately and surely be destined for prison.

Mr. Jones worked hard with both counties to obtain an agreement that would keep Graham out of prison. He believed as we did that Graham had several mental health issues and needed help, not imprisonment. This was a long and arduous journey. Mr. Jones gathered all of Graham's medical records; then we had to wait for the court dates. Not only was the court slow, but just as a court date would come around, Graham would get overwhelmed and be sent to the mental hospital for evaluation and treatment. On more occasions than I can remember, Graham would cut himself and be sent to the state mental hospital. Every visit to the hospital consisted of overmedicating Graham so that he was basically incoherent. He could walk around but barely communicate. Their reasoning was to create a patient who was cooperative with hospital staff. After several days, they would wean Graham off the excess medication in order to regulate the drugs he was prescribed and prepare him to reenter the jail system. The visits never accomplished any understanding or help for Graham, long-term. They just wanted to make him cooperative and stable to go back to jail. The more times he entered the hospital, the more medication he was given to sedate him.

The next two years were filled with great uncertainty. Graham turned nineteen years old in jail. He turned twenty years old in the mental hospital. One particular stay, Graham became extremely paranoid. He called me stating he was frightened to go to sleep. He told me there were two gangs within the hospital staff. Both sides were threatening him. He feared for his life. He had me convinced his life was in danger. I called a meeting with the doctors about my concern. At this visit, Graham told me about how he was hearing voices and watched as the wall was melting in front of him. I was beginning to see the consequences of all the drugs they were giving my son. Instead of realizing they were overmedicating him, the doctors decided to diagnose Graham with schizophrenia. I recognize there are chemical imbalances and diseases where medication is absolutely necessary. These medications can be a miraculous answer for some conditions. Sometimes God uses medication to help and to heal. Sometimes He uses medication to stabilize someone long enough for deep spiritual healing to take place. The problem occurs when we begin to depend on these drugs as if they are God. Our focus should always remain on the Miracle Maker as opposed to the miracle of modern medicine. He will guide us and inform us of our choices. Jesus alone holds all the answers to our struggles. He alone will supply all of our needs in His timing as we continue to look to Him and only Him. We must focus on Jesus.

At this point, I had no control since Graham was legally an adult. The doctors had no answers, so they did what they knew to do, and that was to continue overmedicating Graham. I was afraid for my son's life. I never knew day to day if I would receive a phone call from the jail, the hospital, or the morgue. Every unknown phone call I received for two years had me holding my breath and saying a prayer. Graham was a tortured soul. He had been diagnosed with Asperger syndrome, bipolar disorder, anxiety disorder, and now schizophrenia. He attempted suicide several times. When he wasn't trying to commit suicide, I was scared he would accidently end his life with an overdose or by cutting himself for anxiety relief. How in the world did we get here? I was afraid his life would end too early. I was also afraid he would live but go to prison. Prison was not where he belonged. I knew in my mind that, as a Christian, I should be able to lay this down before the Lord and allow Him to carry me. However, during this time, my faith went back and forth. I had days of big faith and big God thoughts. I also had days of fear and anger. I continued to pray and seek out help through legal and medical means. Most of the time, I felt as if I were being tossed around without any control. Faith is definitely a journey. We don't have to "win" every day. We do need to know that Jesus has already won. He is not keeping count of our wins. I believe God is more concerned about how we are changing along the way than whether or not we are "winning." As my husband says, "It's the fight that counts."

I didn't pretend to have any answers. Being in jail wasn't changing Graham's behavior. The mental health hospitals didn't seem to offer any real help either. Every time he was admitted, they would pump him full of sedatives for several days to calm him down, then build him back up to sobriety and release him back to the jail. No real help was offered. The only real help had to come from Jesus, but how was this to happen? God had told me years ago that Graham was going to get it. Had I really heard this? Maybe Graham would "get it" in heaven. Graham had made a profession of faith and been baptized at seven years old. Only Graham knew if his profession was real. He had never turned his back on his faith. I didn't know what to think. I was so desperate for relief I remember asking God if it wouldn't be better for Him to just take Graham on to heaven. I hated the thought, but I hated the thought of Graham being so miserable too. I begged God to come to the rescue.

My prayers became more and more desperate. During this time, I didn't sleep well. I began waking up in the middle of the night and praying for Graham. I prayed for his safety. I prayed for his protection. I prayed for his rescue. I prayed he wouldn't go to prison. Then I began counting all the scenarios I was afraid of happening. This, I thought, was prayer. I was telling God all the things I didn't want to happen. "Oh God, he just can't go to prison. He's only twenty years old. He is so young and naive. He will most likely be raped, and then he will never be the same again! Graham can't survive eight years in prison. Jesus, you have to change this please."

This went on for several weeks till I realized I was barely sleeping. I was becoming a nervous wreck. My prayers had turned into begging. The only thing this type of praying did for me was make me more fearful and worried. I had to stop. At this realization, when I woke up in the middle of the night, I began saying a simple prayer, "Lord, protect Graham and help me fall back to sleep. Amen." The fearful praying I had been engaging in couldn't be the type of prayer God wanted. As I thought more about my prayers, I suddenly saw them for what they were—worrying and begging. Jesus Himself had said many times that I did not have to worry. I also wasn't meant to be a beggar. I was a child of the Lord Almighty! My prayers needed to change. As I pondered how to change them, I remembered what a dear friend asked me a few months earlier. She asked, "What do you want for Graham?" That question made me boil all my wants down to two things: peace and joy. Graham had been so anxious and so depressed for so long. That isn't what God intended for him. Jeremiah 29:11 tells me that God has a future and a hope for us. Job 8:21 tells me that God Himself wants to fill our mouths with laughter and our lips with shouts of joy. He wants hope, peace, and joy for Graham. That became my prayer. I prayed, "God, dispel and cast out the spirit of depression and anxiety that resides in Graham. Lord, replace these voids now with Your Spirit of joy and peace." After that simple prayer, I praised God. It wasn't long before most of my prayer time was just praise and worship. My sleepless nights, my anxiety, my fear, my worry went away as I purposefully cast my cares on Christ. It was an amazing time of growth for me as a believer in Christ and as a mom. It became a time of freedom.

I was experiencing God in a new way. He wasn't someone I needed to beg or inform. He knew everything and desired to give good gifts. My encounters with Jesus began to transform my thinking and my life. Then it dawned on me: it is encountering Jesus that changes us. He, and He alone, is joy and peace. I know I had been taught that. I had probably even said that to people. But now God had explained it to me. Now God had brought me personally to that place of experiencing Him in a new way so that now I could enjoy Him as the Person of peace. That was a revelation to me. And that revelation changed my prayers. Now I added, "God, let Graham experience You in a way that only You know he needs and that will blow his mind. He needs You." My faith gauge shot up as well as my peace level. No matter what the situation looked like, God was able to change it all in an instant. Graham had to be brought to the point of belief and surrender to God. He had gotten to a place in his life where he believed the drugs were his answer to having peace. He was surrendering to drugs and cutting. But those are just counterfeits for the real thrill, the real comfort that only Jesus brings. Graham needed to encounter the real Jesus, say yes to him, and surrender to him. I also had to believe that God could take care of Graham wherever he was. If he was in prison, then God would be there. If going to prison was what it took for Graham to experience Jesus as his peace and his joy, then it would be worth it. I felt myself encountering the real Jesus, saying yes to Him, and surrendering fully to Him.

One and a half years after being arrested at the local grocery store, Graham's attorney, Mr. Jones, managed to get approval from both counties to send Graham to a state-funded rehabilitation program. This was a place of incarceration, yet it was also a program for addicts. I could see God was working. When he completed this six-month program, Graham would be released from the impending doom of prison. I was so relieved. This was a move of God through Mr. Jones. After six months in rehabilitation, then Graham would go into a transition home for a few months and then be free. Finally, good news! I knew Graham's problems were more than an addiction to drugs. He had high anxiety and depression, which only Jesus could take away.

Graham was taken to the rehabilitation program and admitted to the section that was dedicated as medical. This meant he would be watched over by a medical staff. This was a great relief to me. The staff would make sure he received all his medication. By this time, Graham was taking a lot of medications. Most were for anxiety, some for bipolar/schizophrenia disorder, as well as a sleeping aid. It comforted me to know he was in the medical area of the program. Halfway through the program, we traveled to visit Graham for the second time.

The first visit had gone very well. Graham seemed more relaxed and was fitting in well. However, at this second visit, we were told Graham was not available to visit us in the public visiting area. After a long wait, we were finally able to see him in a private room, where we could only visit him behind glass. He was somewhat sedated, and he looked terribly disheveled. Graham also had a large bandage on his wrist. Because of the sedation, I wasn't able to get the answers to all my questions. The staff cited confidentiality and would not share information with us.

Shortly afterward, Graham was returned to jail. They returned him to the original county jail. This was the county that wanted to send him to prison for eight years. I was horrified to discover that the so-called medical staff at rehabilitation had not been giving Graham his medication on a daily basis. If he overslept, he did not receive his medication. Apparently, they insisted it was Graham's responsibility to be awake at the proper time. He would beg for his prescribed drugs, but the staff refused. Without his medication, Graham's anxiety got the best of him again. He managed to obtain a razor blade and cut his wrist badly. The staff stabilized and isolated him. They then proceeded to send him back to jail, stating they were not capable of housing an inmate who was suicidal. The most appalling information was that the county considered this leaving of the facility as a nonfulfillment of his sentence. Now eight years in prison was back in play. The reason Graham was not able to fulfill his commitment wasn't his fault. He needed his medications, and they intentionally withheld them from him. My faith in God and His purposes for us was tested once again. I asked God to intervene and prohibit Graham from being sent to prison. However, after all I had learned, I stuck mostly to praying for Graham to experience Jesus as his one and only peace and joy. I had to check my feelings constantly and allow my faith to outrun my feelings of despair.

I also shared every step of my journey with my trusted Christian sisters. They would pray with me and encourage me. God showed me the reality of Revelation 12:11: "They triumphed over him [the devil] by the blood of the Lamb and by the word of their testimony." As I continued to tell our story, my struggles, and the insights God was giving me along the way, I could feel my faith grow and strengthen. As I walked through my struggles honestly with my friends and gave God glory along the way, the enemy was overcome.

We managed to secure Mr. Jones as Graham's attorney again. He subpoenaed Graham's records from the rehabilitation unit. Although this took a couple of months, the records did confirm Graham was not given his medication. This was then argued as the reason he could not complete the program. We finally had our day in court. As Michael and I waited in the courtroom, we prayed. I had everyone I knew praying. We waited for them to escort Graham into the room. Suddenly the side door opened, and an officer escorted several handcuffed inmates into the room. When my eyes laid hold of my Graham, he was wearing an orange jumpsuit. His hair was sticking out in every direction. His facial expression was blank. He was scary-looking. I remember whispering to Michael, "I'm so glad God doesn't give us glimpses of the future. If I had a sneak peek of this when Graham was younger, I would have been terrified. I would have lived my life and parented out of fear. God is so good."

Mr. Jones managed to obtain an audience with the judge just prior to walking into court. As it turns out, God gave Graham a judge who was familiar with Asperger syndrome. When he read of the incompetency of the rehabilitation program, the judge called me and his dad to the front of the courtroom. Amazingly, the prosecution still argued that Graham did not complete his rehabilitation and deserved to begin his eight-year sentence in prison. The judge asked me as mom if I had anything to say. Now after two full years of jail time, I was grateful Graham was still alive. I was grateful for the judge, and I was grateful for this opportunity to speak. With tears, I told the judge that Graham had committed crimes but that he had been in jail for two years now. I said, "During that time, he has cut himself more times than I can count." I held my son's arm up to show all his scars. "My son has mental issues that prison will not help. Even the medical rehabilitation didn't serve Graham properly. Please let him come home so we as his family can begin to really help him." The Lord God was in that courtroom that day. The judge said, "I will never send another person to that rehabilitation program." He counted Graham's time spent incarcerated and declared that he had served his sentence and would now be released.

I was overjoyed and a little in shock! We had managed to get Graham released from jail shortly before his twenty-first birthday. He had spent his eighteenth birthday in jail after his first arrest. After the second arrest, he spent his nineteenth birthday in jail and his twentieth birthday in a mental hospital. But Graham would not be spending his twenty-first birthday in prison, thanks to God's protection. We didn't have any amazing plan for Graham when he returned home. I just continued to pray for God to turn his anxiety into peace, his depression into joy, and for Graham to experience God Himself. Now the next leg of the journey started, and the thought began to sink in: *What in the world will we experience next?*

Taken first week Graham returned home from jail.
(left to right) Titus, Graham, Jake, Blake

CHAPTER 8

Coming Home

When Graham was released from jail, we were living in a home already too small for our family of five people and two dogs. Adding Graham, a self-professed loner, to a crowded home would prove to be more than difficult. As always, God came to the rescue through one of my dear friends, Sharon and her husband, Ben. They had an old pop-up camper they didn't use anymore. Once Sharon learned of our tight quarters and Graham's idiosyncrasies, she and Ben generously offered us their camper. We were overjoyed for Graham to have a room of his own. Having a private place to retreat to would help Graham and us deal better with any frustration that was bound to arise. It was one seemingly small yet very big provision of our God.

The first month went as well, as can be expected. We were all trying to be positive and helpful to one another. Graham, although not a clean freak by any stretch of the imagination, did his best to clean up after himself in the kitchen. And he loved having his own place to crash whenever he needed. It wasn't long, though, before anxiety showed its ugly head. One particular night, Graham was pacing frantically and showing signs of being overwhelmed. It happened just like it used to at bed time. Michael and I headed to bed as we encouraged Graham to take his sleeping pill and lie down so he could fall asleep. He continued to pace. Not long after we had gone to bed, Graham came in, pacing, wide-eyed, and talking about having a panic attack. We stayed calm and prayed over him. So as to not give the panic attack too much attention, we encouraged him to take his sleeping aid and go straight to his bed and read or just rest. Amazingly, he did just that. Michael and I prayed again and tried to go to sleep too. I lay awake praying for peace to fall on Graham and for his anxiety to be overcome with the presence of Jesus. The night came and went without incident. Apparently, Graham did manage to overcome that night, which strengthened him for all the nights to come. Maybe he was finally learning to cope against his anxiety attacks.

After about six weeks, Graham began connecting with some old friends. They would pick him up and take him into town, where he would hang out in Austin's Zilker Park. Soon he would disappear for the entire weekend. Of course, this made us nervous, thinking he was getting involved with the wrong people and possibly using drugs again. However, he would return by Monday and say he just hung out. It wasn't long though that after one such weekend, he didn't return home. I did the familiar act of calling the hospitals and the jail. To my relief, he wasn't in either place. We continued to carry on with life as usual, praying for his safe return.

A week went by when Michael and I decided to view his bank card usage. We were able to determine he was in north Austin. He hadn't called us for help, but we were convinced if we did not intervene, we could lose him again. Michael and I took our two younger sons Titus (seventeen) and Blake (fourteen) and became detectives in north Austin, which was an hour's drive from our home. We began at the last place his bank card had been used and followed the trail from there. I had a picture of Graham on my phone that I showed to people, asking them if they had seen my son. It was a surreal experience. Some said no. Some said they had seen him but didn't know where he was now. Others looked at me and said, "This is your son? I thought he was just some homeless guy." I found that interesting. Isn't every homeless guy a son to someone? We came across some homeless men under a small bridge off the beaten path. They were drinking and talking as we cautiously walked up to them. I caught myself looking at these guys differently. We asked them if they had seen Graham. Who was their mother? Had anyone ever looked for them? Did they feel as if anyone cared for them? I was even more determined to find my son and show him no matter what he ever does or doesn't do, he is my son and I will always love him. That decision had been made in a jail cell in Branson, Missouri, five years earlier.

One of the store clerks to whom we showed Graham's picture was a young girl who couldn't have been more than twenty-one years old. She looked at me with great surprise and told me that she ran away from home when she was sixteen years old and her mom never came looking for her. I didn't know what to say. Compassion welled up inside me for this poor girl. Of course, I didn't know all the circumstances. Maybe she was abused at home, or maybe she had a great home but was just a rebellious teen. Whatever the case, Jesus wanted her to know that she was wanted. She was loved. I wanted to hug her close and mother her. I wanted to tell her how much God loved her and that she was worthy of being sought after. But I didn't know how to do that at the time. I just told her, "I'm sorry."

The man at the local thrift store said there was a homeless guy in the back alley sleeping behind a Dumpster. We thought it could be him. We hoped it was him so we could take him home where he belonged. As we approached the sleeping man, who was under some old blankets, he jumped up and apologized for being there. It wasn't Graham. We then showed him Graham's picture and asked the same question we had been asking all afternoon, "Have you seen our son?" This fellow looked hard at the picture then asked if we were the police. Funny that anyone would take a look at our little family and think *cops*. Once we convinced him we weren't the police, he let his guard down and said he had seen Graham. Tim, which was his name, wouldn't say where he had seen Graham because he was afraid of upsetting me. He seemed very nice and sincere. He wanted to protect me, a mom, from being hurt and afraid. I told him I believed the Lord would provide everything that I needed to get through this. He enthusiastically shared that he knew Jesus as well. Once he felt safe with us, he told us his name and his story. He was recently released from prison and was on his way back to his ex-wife and child.

After some coaxing, Tim told us that Graham was at a crack house a couple of miles from there. He explained that the boy was introduced to heroine and reluctantly participated. Now he was in this crack house and was probably pretty messed up. After I caught my breath, the five of us drove to the house. We bought Tim some food and thanked him for his help. Before deciding our next step, all five of us stood in the mini-mart parking lot, held hands in a circle, and prayed. We prayed thanking God for leading us to Tim. We prayed for Tim and his reunion with his family. Then Tim prayed for us. He prayed for Graham's safe return home. It was again a surreal experience holding hands with this homeless fellow and praying for Graham.

Tim seemed very protective of us. He was especially concerned for my safety. He said, "This drug guy hates women. If you walk up to his door, he will likely go off on you. Promise me you won't go up to that door." I promised, but we had to do something. Fearing violence, we decided to let Tim go to the door while we waited across the street. Someone answered the door and talked with Tim. He was told that the main drug guy and Graham had gone somewhere and would be back soon.

The only thing we could do was to wait. We hugged Tim good-bye and made a plan from there.

Michael, Titus, Blake, and I decided to stake out the crack house. We parked across the street and waited. We discussed what we should do. If this guy was dangerous and if he wanted to keep a hold of Graham, we needed to make a desperate plan. If Graham was under the influence of drugs, he would most likely not cooperate, making our plans even harder to accomplish. We made a brave plan to intercept their car as soon as they drove up. Michael and Titus would jump out and grab Graham, forcing him into our car. I would then speed off just like in the movies. As we sat there waiting, the ridiculousness of the situation did not escape us. We even said, "I can't believe we are holed up across the street from a crack house!" We laughed to keep from being overwhelmed with the situation. All the while, I knew my God was big. My God answered prayers. Come what may, I had to keep my eyes focused on God and His abilities while keeping my feet ready to jump out and grab Graham.

After three hours of no movement at the house, we checked Graham's bank card again to see where they might be and if they were close to being back to the house. We discovered Graham's card had just been used at the Taco Bell two miles away. What should we do? If we left, we could miss him arriving at the house. But if we caught him away from the house, that would be easier and safer. We decided to leave Michael and Titus on the curb while Blake and I went to Taco Bell. I was ready to speed back to the house if/when Michael called with news that they had arrived back at the house. Maybe not the safest thing for Michael and Titus, but it was our best plan at the time.

Blake and I arrived at the restaurant. There was no sign of the drug dealer's car. Showing Graham's picture from my phone again, we asked the people behind the counter if they had seen Graham. They did not remember seeing him. I didn't know if this was Graham we were chasing or someone who had stolen his bank card. I called Michael to give him an update. Tim had walked back by and told them that the guys in the house had spotted them across the street. They were thinking Michael and Titus might be undercover cops, so they were walking around the block. Before we left, I went to the restroom. Blake waited for me at the end of the hallway in the restaurant. It was going to be dark soon, making this adventure very dangerous. We would need to decide our next plan of action. As I came out of the bathroom, I heard Blake exclaim, "Graham!" I looked up to see Graham walking out of the men's room right in front of me. He was looking at Blake and said, "Blake!" Then in utter astonishment I said, "Graham!" To which he turned and said, "Mom!" We all stood there for a few seconds in silence; then we laughed at the humor of the situation. A million things went through my head. Was the drug guy in the bathroom? Did Graham want to see us? Was he under the influence of some drug right now? Was he hurt? Why did he just disappear? Why hadn't he called us? But all I managed to say was, "Are you okay?" He said, "Yeah." I asked, "Are you ready to go home?" He simply replied,

"Yes." We got into the car, picked up Michael and Titus, and went home.

As it turns out, Tim had been wrong. Graham had never been in that crack house. Graham had not tried heroine that week. He said he just lost his ride home and decided to hang out in north Austin for a while. I may never understand why he did that or why he didn't call us. I was, however, aware that God was ever before us, watching over Graham. We laughed all the way home about staking out the crack house and having a plan to kidnap Graham. Graham laughed and said we were crazy. *We* were crazy?

CHAPTER 9

The Sandwich

That summer, Graham turned twenty-one years old. This was his first birthday in four years where he was at home and not in the hospital or jail. It was a joyous birthday dinner with the whole family together. The last three years had been terrifying and faith producing. We were all thanking God those years were over. We weren't sure where Graham would go from here, but the last few months at home were good. He was taking his medications properly, handling anxiety well, and back to being a part of the family. I was, however, very nervous about his going to downtown Austin every weekend. I didn't believe he was ready to face old temptations so soon.

After one such weekend, it was already Monday afternoon, and Graham had not made it home yet. I was at work and had just entered an important meeting when I received a call from a local hospital. The nurse said Graham had been admitted to the hospital the night before. The only thing she could tell me over the phone was that he was in stable condition and we needed to come to the hospital. I called Michael, who was available to go immediately. As I went into my meeting, I wondered the whole time, *What now? Has he overdosed accidently? Has he gotten into a fight and gotten hurt? Did he actually try to hurt himself again?* Past history convinced me it was one of those three explanations.

Two hours later, Michael called. He was at the hospital with Graham and had talked with the nurse at length. He now had Graham and was on his way home. It turns out that none of what I was thinking explained Graham's latest hospital stay. The night before, while hanging out in Austin, Graham had been with a group of friends and had left his wallet in someone's apartment. While they were out and about late, Graham decided he was hungry. But he didn't have his money with him. Being the inventive guy he is, Graham took a sharp object and cut his ankle. He actually cut it badly enough for several stitches. Then he walked into the emergency room of the nearest hospital. While they were stitching his ankle, he asked for a sandwich because he was hungry. This hospital apparently has seen the homeless pull this trick time and time again. They denied him a sandwich in hopes to deter such stunts in the future.

They had not bargained on Graham's insistence. He felt wronged. He felt angry because they should care for him. He felt hungry! Graham proceeded to yell and knock over trays. He became so disruptive they sedated him to such an extent that he was asleep fourteen hours later. Graham ended up spending the night and half of Monday in the hospital. That's when the hospital staff called me to come pick him up as they were ready to discharge him. I'm sure they eventually had to feed him.

Now I ask you, Wouldn't it have been better to have given the boy a sandwich? I'm sure they spent more money on his medication and overnight stay than if they had just given him a sandwich. To this day, when we learn someone is in the hospital, someone in our family asks, "Why? Were they hungry?"

CHAPTER 10

Going Out on His Own

We knew Graham couldn't live with us forever. But I wasn't sure he could function successfully on his own. I did believe that if we were nearby to help him adjust and learn to live on his own, in time he would be completely successful. We needed to find a good place for Graham to live and become more independent. Because of his diagnoses, he had qualified for a monthly Social Security check. He had applied for Social Security back when he was living with Grandma. They had him visit several doctors who did agree with the diagnoses he had received while in jail. He jumped through all the hoops and had been approved after his first application. Once Graham was released from jail, it didn't take long to get his payments reinstated. We began visiting all the low-income housing we could find in Austin. After a little research, Graham and I visited several apartments where he met all the qualifications. I was particularly hoping and praying for an apartment we had visited near Zilker Park. They were new apartments. The residents lived independently; however, the staff were available to keep an eye out for them and even act as their caseworker if needed. This seemed perfect to me. Graham wasn't excited but had no objections. We were able to get his name on the waiting list. They estimated a three- to six-month wait.

If I could just get him in his own apartment, I thought, *maybe he would be okay.* However, the residential complex soon called to inform me they could not accept Graham because of his felony. This was the last straw. Where in all the world would he go? If he couldn't qualify for transitional-type housing, how would he transition? How could I ever help him? How was God going to fix this? I was mad at the system and feeling defeated again. Home was tight quarters physically and not a relaxing environment. I came home one day to find that Graham had an old high school friend over for dinner. Then he explained to me his friend needed a place to live. Graham thought it would be perfect for his friend to stay with us. Life was about to get more intense. This was very much like Graham to be generous and wanting to help his friends. I've always loved this aspect of Graham's personality. It gave me hope for the compassion that God had placed somewhere deep inside Graham. We, of course, received Cody with open arms. *Oh my goodness!* I thought. *Will I have a nervous breakdown before this is all over?*

After five months of being home, Graham and Cody decided they preferred living a homeless lifestyle near Zilker Park. Nothing we could say would convince Graham otherwise. The fifth month after being released from jail, Graham was officially living homeless. He would call occasionally or drop by my office in Austin. He was happy to be on the streets and free, but he was still anxious. Graham was convinced that all he needed was to smoke marijuana daily to take care of his anxiety. He wanted to go to Colorado where it was legal. I knew God had Graham. I should have learned by now that I couldn't control the situation. In fact, I didn't want to try controlling it anymore. My controlling never really worked. The only thing I seemed to receive out of trying to control Graham's situations was worry and fear. A month into his homelessness, I sat in my office watching Graham pace back and forth, talking about how he just needed to get to Colorado. I knew he must go and experience for himself. No coaxing, informing, or begging was going to change his mind. I suddenly found myself saying, "Graham, if you want to go so badly, you should purchase a bus ticket with your next check and go."

I think he just wanted the vote of confidence that he could do this. Within the next few days, Graham's government check arrived, and he was back in my office, purchasing a one-way ticket to Denver, Colorado. I did tell him it wouldn't be easy. I told him I wished he would wait till Michael and I could go with him and set him up with resources (even though I had no idea when we would have the financial resources to do that). I encouraged him to consider all the medications he was taking and ask himself how he would get those refilled in a strange town. Nothing was going to stop Graham from this new adventure. Now you may ask yourself, How does a kid with Asperger syndrome just up and move that far away from his family and friends? I just don't know. I do know Asperger looks very different in each person. Graham has always enjoyed experiencing something new. However, it had to be on his schedule and under his planning. Graham hates surprises!

Within three days, Graham was off to the bus station. He had his identification, flip phone, backpack, bank card, medications, and a few sets of clothes. As mom, I had all sorts of thoughts. I understood the desire as a young person to be independent and adventurous. I remember having that feeling when I was twenty. I was also very glad that despite the Asperger's diagnosis, Graham possessed this adventurous spirit. But Graham still possessed many AS traits that could inhibit his coping in the world alone. He didn't have natural understanding of interactions with people and social cues. Although he had experienced so much in his short life, he was still immature and innocent in many ways. I didn't want people to take advantage of him. I didn't want his medications to run out, causing him to have a massive panic attack and decide to do something that would end in jail or, worse, in his death. As I considered all the possibilities, I remembered my prayer nights from when he was on his way to prison. I remembered what God had taught me and what I had experienced when I had focused on Jesus and rested in the Father. So every day, I made that same decision. I worshipped God. I focused on His goodness and not only His *ability* to care for my son but His *desire* to care for him.

Graham waving goodbye as he heads to the bus station.

I was determined to trust Jesus and send Graham off with my support. We made plans to go out to dinner as a family, have a few laughs, get a good night's sleep, and then off to the bus station in the morning. Have I mentioned how Graham always wants to make all the plans no matter how great your plans sound? I was disappointed but not surprised when he informed us that he would spend his last night in a homeless camp. "After all, I have a lot of friends in the park I need to say good-bye to," he reasoned. So I dropped Graham off at the park before I headed to work. I called him the next day when he was scheduled to be boarding his bus. Someone answered, but it wasn't Graham. After they hung up on me, I tried calling again several times, but no one ever answered again. Once again, I had no idea of Graham's location. I questioned whether he had made it to the bus station or if he had been mugged. The next day, I even called several hospitals. Thankfully, he wasn't there. I didn't call the jail. I was afraid of what I might hear if I called the jail.

It was a couple of days later when Graham called, telling us how someone had stolen his phone the night before he left for Colorado. He managed to board the bus, make it to Denver, and purchase another phone. I admit during this time, I was experiencing a feeling of relief. I was relieved to have my house back. I was relieved to have my privacy back. I fought back the feeling of guilt. A month later, Graham called to inform us that Colorado was not what he had thought it would be. There were so many rules associated with his so-called freedom. So now he was headed to Portland. He had Facebook friends there who would put him to work trimming cannabis. He even had a friend to travel with him. Jeff was an older man who was also on medications, and supposedly, he had friends in Portland too. They set off hitchhiking together from Denver to Portland in October.

Now, part of me was relieved Graham had a buddy with him. The much bigger part of me was very concerned. Who was Jeff? What kind of mental issues did he have? I watch crime shows, and my imagination could wander, to say the least. Every day, I had a choice. Was I going to focus on the situation at hand or on my God? For the most part, I remember throwing myself into my work; and when I didn't have a task at hand, I chose to worship. God really does inhabit the praises of His people! Actively, intentionally focusing on God the Father, Jesus, and the Holy Spirit brought me peace.

Several days passed, and Graham called again. He told me the story of how he and Jeff remembered that the mental hospitals in this country are usually very happy to provide you with a bus ticket anywhere you want to go if you tell them you have people waiting for you there. I suppose that is an attempt to get people back together with loved ones who may want to help them, or maybe it is their only way of getting these patients out of their system. Whatever the reason, they knew it to be true, so that was their motive in entering this hospital in Northern Colorado. Graham told me the hospital gave him a bus ticket to Portland, and he was on his way now. When I asked about

Jeff, Graham chuckled and said, "Oh, they decided to keep him." Was that God's protection over Graham or God's sense of humor? I may never know. But for that moment, we chose to laugh.

CHAPTER 11

Relaxing Trip to Cabo

During this time in our lives, God had me placed in a wonderful position as executive director of a local ministry. There, I was challenged professionally, loved personally, and protected spiritually. The center was volunteer-driven, and I had the best volunteers to be found anywhere. A couple of supporters of the ministry generously offered me and my husband a two-week stay in Cabo San Lucas, Mexico, including airfare. This was a dream come true for us. Our boys at home were cared for, and Graham was on his way to Portland, Oregon, where he hoped to have friends and a job waiting for him. Off to Cabo we went for a little R & R.

The second day in Cabo, we were settling in nicely when we received a call from Portland, Oregon. It was Graham, and he was in a hospital. He ran out of all his antipsychotic medications, so he decided to walk into the nearest hospital and ask for help. At first, he wanted medications, but they refused him. He began to realize he wasn't with anyone who knew his mental history, so he began telling them his story. The more he talked, the more panicked he became. The hospital did not consider him a threat to himself or others, so they would not admit him as a patient. I'm sure Graham fought hard for help, but they would not reconsider. He wasn't familiar with being refused. Graham usually manipulated people until he received exactly what he wanted. I'm sure he pulled out all the stops as he did when he wanted that sandwich in the Austin hospital. This time, he couldn't manipulate them. Graham called me desperately, wanting me to say something that would change their minds, but there was nothing I could do or say to help. I talked with the social worker in the hospital who couldn't offer any help. I tried giving Graham some encouragement and guidance, but he didn't want to hear anything I had to say. He eventually became very angry with me and hung up. I called the hospital back. They said he had left. Before he hung up, Graham became desperate and hysterical, saying, "I'm gonna hurt somebody." He was completely out of his medications, and I feared for his life. He had lost his phone, and now I had no way to contact him.

Through all the years with Graham and all the trials, this was the time I felt the most helpless. I didn't know where he was. I had no one to call. I couldn't even hop in the car or a plane and go find him. It was as if God Himself had picked me up and dropped me off where I had absolutely no way to intervene. I was in Mexico. Graham was in Oregon. Now what would I do? I was not so naive to believe this could not be the end. In fact, I knew that was a real possibility.

Would Graham finally take his own life? Would he hurt someone else and end up in the dreaded prison I had fought so hard to keep him out of? I hung up the phone. With tears in my eyes and an exhausted spirit, I prayed with my husband. I found myself in the familiar place of choice. Horrible thoughts of what might happen tried to consume me. Would I let them consume me, or would I choose to rest in His perfect peace? I had to choose once again to believe God loved Graham more than I did. I believed God was with Graham, and He knew this would happen and that I would not be available to help. I knew that Graham had free choice, but my God would do everything possible to reach him. I focused on the fact that I can trust God even if this turned out to be the end. I chose to believe His character was only good. I chose to worship Him. Then I fell asleep in the sun, poolside.

I am still in awe of the peace that God gave me that day. That is the peace that passes all understanding. This peace hadn't come to me overnight. It hadn't come without a process. It wasn't just given to me. *I had to choose it.* There had been so many times I did not choose to rest in God's peace. But then again, He was patiently teaching me. I *had* chosen it over and over again until the one time that I needed it more than ever. God came through with such a peace that I fell asleep! And I'm not even a nap person. To me, that's a miracle. I soon found out it was just one miracle of many more to come.

CHAPTER 12

The Turning Point

We arrived home two weeks after the infamous phone call from Graham. We had heard nothing from Graham during these two weeks. It was a Wednesday when we arrived home, and I was registered for a women's conference that weekend. I remember telling Michael that we would have to fly to Portland and become detectives again to find him if he didn't call us by the time I got back from the retreat. I was hoping we wouldn't have to stake out a crack house again. But deep inside, I knew it could be much worse than staking out a crack house. Someone, meaning well, said to me, "Well, no news is good news." But I knew that wasn't true. Without identification, my son could be in the morgue, his body waiting to be identified. How would this play out? How would I respond? I didn't know how I would respond to such horrible news, but I knew right now I was going to respond by once again choosing to trust my loving God no matter what the circumstances. This was the point at which I had to face the fact that this journey could be over. There was a real possibility that Graham was no longer alive. Graham as a baby and little boy played in my memory like a home movie. He was such a curious, funny little boy. I don't know why all our dreams for him had not turned out the way we wanted. I believe we were the best parents we knew how to be. We raised Graham to know Jesus. We made more mistakes than I could ever count, but we always loved him. We always forgave him. We always gave him another chance. We never gave up on him.

If this was the end, I would need to choose to trust God. I know God's character says He always loved and never gave up on Graham. I chose to believe the profession of faith Graham made for Christ at seven years old was true. Graham would live eternally with God in heaven. God gave Graham free will. Graham chose drugs, anger, and manipulation for the answer to his problems instead of running to Jesus. Eventually that would catch up with him and prove to be an ultimately destructive path. Whatever the end result of this journey, this fight, I would choose God. I would not blame God but thank Him for fighting for and pursuing Graham. I would choose to praise God and tell Graham's story in order to show others that no matter what, God is good.

Amazingly, I managed to enjoy the women's retreat. It was short, beginning Friday afternoon and ending Saturday evening. As soon as the last song was sung, I turned my phone back on, and my thoughts went back to Graham. I wondered if we would be booking a flight to Portland in the next couple of days. As I watched my phone boot up, it immediately began to ring. It was an unidentified number from California. I stared at it and thought, *That's one state over from Oregon. I wonder.* I answered, and from the other end, I heard Graham's voice, "Hi, Mom." I was speechless. Tears filled my eyes, and my heart beat faster. It wasn't over! Graham was actually cheery. My mind went back to that Taco Bell when he walked out of the bathroom after we had searched high and low for him. I didn't know what to say first. I was so happy he was alive. I think my first words were, "Graham, I haven't heard from you in over two weeks!" He quickly said, "I know, Mom. I'm sorry." Did Graham just say, "I'm sorry"? I asked if he was okay. He told me he was better than he had ever been. He told me he loved absolutely everyone, and he was at peace. I wondered what drug he was on now, but I wanted desperately to believe it was God who had gotten a hold of him.

Graham proceeded to tell me the story. This was the event that God had been building up to all along. I paced while I listened and interacted with him as all the women at the conference hugged good-bye and packed their cars. I wanted to scream, "Hey, don't ya'll know a miracle is being told here?" I was in awe. I'm sure I will not get all the details correct, but I know the major highlights. Graham left the hospital where I had last talked with him. He later met up with a few other homeless people. They all decided to hop trains down to

California. So Graham and his new buddies did just that (it's funny to me now that my son hopping trains is not a big deal to me). Somewhere along the way as Graham slept, someone with him stole his backpack, which was everything he owned. He expressed to me that when he woke up and discovered his pack and buddies missing, he suddenly felt all alone. He was wearing summer clothes in Northern California and was freezing. I'll never forget Graham asking me, "When I woke up and my bag was stolen, you know what I did, Mom?" I said, "Graham, there is no telling what you did." The next words out of his mouth astounded me. "I forgave them. I'll never know who did it, and I just forgave them. Then I realized I didn't know anyone for thousands of miles. But I did know God was there, so I prayed." I listened in amazement as he told me how he went to church right away and how God, through the church, gave him a phone, a backpack, a change of clothes, and a scooter. He didn't credit the church for this. He directly credited God. I pinched myself. Was this real? Did God get a hold of Graham and turn this high tide of hopelessness in a blink of an eye?

I have often told people that story of how God met Graham at just the right moment. That was the moment Graham was receptive. God knew when that moment was coming. God built up all of Graham's circumstances to that perfect moment. God waited patiently for Graham to come to that moment of decision. He knew I would need to be out of the picture. He knew exactly what Graham needed. And what Graham needed was to be all alone. All alone that is except for the presence of

God. Graham recognized the presence of God. But first he recognized the absence of everyone else. How many times do I get in the way of God working His miracles with my children, my husband, or my friends? I have thanked Him a million times, and I will thank Him a million more for picking me up and getting me out of the country; thus, out of the way for Graham to feel alone enough to reach out to God. I find it amazing that at the time Graham was feeling all alone, that was the moment in Cabo that I was feeling the total, peaceful presence of God. Graham also recognized God's presence after he recognized that there was no one else on whom he could call to rescue him.

As I was preparing to write this part of Graham's story, God turned the focus on me. He asked me, "When do you run to people or things or even yourself before running to Me?" In the light of how Graham came back to Christ, I am convicted to think about the areas in my life where God is trying to get my attention, but instead of looking to Him, I look to my husband. I look to my dear friends. They are wonderful, and they are God's gift to me, but my *first* love, the one I *first* run to, should be Jesus. After all, isn't He the ultimate and best choice? I want to run to the best One first, not last or even second.

Graham later conveyed the rest of his story. It was during this time that God gave Graham a twofold vision. He showed Graham a picture of the rest of his life without God. It was filled with distress, anxiety, and destruction. He then showed

Graham a picture of the rest of his life with God. This life was filled with peace, joy, and love. God then asked Graham to decide which life he wanted to walk. Graham chose life, love, peace, and joy. Graham chose God.

CHAPTER 13

Personal Faith

Now I would like to say that after the experience on the streets of California where Graham lost everything and found Jesus's presence and the power of forgiveness, it was smooth sailing from there, but it wasn't. He did become a part of the church that had received him and provided for him. He went to Bible studies and made friends. Graham even found a place to live, but his home was miles from the church. Because of a lack of transportation, he didn't make it to church very often, but things were definitely looking up. His life was different. Only time would tell if what he had experienced was a real and permanent life change.

Graham had not been successful in obtaining his antipsychotic medications, but he was successful in obtaining a medical marijuana card. The fact that Graham was completely off all his medications was amazing. I wondered if he would eventually have a breakdown and need his medications again. He smoked his medical marijuana daily. I am not a proponent of marijuana. However, I had seen my child live in constant anxiety, go through several panic attacks, and many suicide attempts. He had been in and out of the state hospital more times than I could remember. He believed this "natural drug" was going to help him cope. Secretly, I guess I did too. Of course, more than anything, I preferred for God to swoop in and save the day as He seemed to have done on the streets several months earlier. Graham did seem to be coping. Until one day.

I received a call from Graham three months after his connection with the church in Sacramento, California. He said, "Mom, tell me the truth. Don't lie to me. I can take it." Well, of course, I will always tell the truth. What in the world was Graham thinking about now? He proceeded to explain how he had been reading his birth certificate, and Michael's birth date was incorrect. He knew he had been born in a different state than his brothers, so now he needed to know one thing. "Is Dad my real dad?" he asked with the determination to get the truth out of me. "Of course, he is your biological dad, Graham," I stated, astonished that he would ask such a question. He was not convinced. I had to swear to him that I was telling the truth. If he had a different dad, I would certainly tell him. "Your daddy is the only man I have ever been with, son, I promise. We don't lie to you." I spoke to him with compassion and as much persuasion as I could muster. He finally said okay.

A few days later, he called again with questions about a different religion and telling me maybe we've had it wrong all along. Now I began to think he had gotten involved in a cult. *For goodness sake*, I thought, *is there anything this boy won't experience?* A few days later, he called again in a full-blown panic attack. He was crying, saying he didn't even know if he was alive or dead. He was thinking maybe he was already in hell. He was afraid that this life was not real, but actually he was in hell and would wake up any minute and realize that he was in hell. Graham was terrified and crying out for our help. I wasn't sure what drug he was on or what group he was associating with, but thank God he was calling us. My heart hurt for him. I tried to speak truth to him, but I wasn't sure he was in the frame of mind to receive it. I lavished my love on him through my words and through scripture that came to my mind.

I remembered how God had taken hold of Graham's attention when we were not available to intervene that fateful day several months ago. I also remembered that although God has His perfect plan, He also gives Graham a say in his own life. He had choices to make. I felt strongly this was a good time for us to help, but Graham had to make that decision. I carefully asked, "Graham, it sounds like you need us to come be with you for a while. I would be happy to make that happen. You tell me. Would you like me to come visit you?" He paused and simply but coherently said, "I want Dad." Now, you might think him wanting his dad would have made me feel left out, especially after I had just offered my help. On the contrary, I was overjoyed. I didn't think Michael could actually take off work whereas I could manage it. However, when I heard Graham ask for a visit from his dad, I quickly but calmly said, "Then we will make that happen." As I handed the phone over to Michael, I informed him that Graham needed and wanted a visit from him. Michael was as full of joy over this request as I was.

Within two days, Michael was in California, loving on Graham. He didn't find a hospital. He didn't obtain a counselor. He just spoke into his son's life as only a father can. Michael spent a week with Graham. We soon found out Graham was not involved in a cult. I think ultimately he was very lonely and smoking too much marijuana. As Michael spent time with Graham, he noticed Graham didn't smoke once while he was with him. I guess he didn't need to smoke. *His dad was present.* They went to his church, and Michael met his roommate. The best of their time together was spent hiking in Yosemite National Park. I know Michael gave Graham the best thing a parent can give their child. He spoke affirmation into him. Every chance Michael got, he told Graham how very proud of him he was. He told him he could be successful living on his own. A wonderful father told his son over and over again that God was with him and for him. Michael assured Graham that Mom and Dad believed in him too. Michael assured Graham that God was inside him and with him through everything. They discussed how God had a purpose and a plan for Graham. They prayed together. A father prayed over his son.

Sometime during that week, Graham returned to normal. His panic and crazy thoughts were gone. All he needed was time with his daddy, time with someone who cared for him and poured into him the love he needed. I'm sure Graham smoked again at some point after that visit, but he was recentered that week by the love of his earthly dad. Michael left to come home with complete confidence that Graham was well cared for by his Heavenly Father. I have not seen Graham in a full-blown panic attack since then.

Two months later, Graham was doing well alone. He was attending church when he was able to obtain a ride and trying everything he could do to get a job. That month, my church had an encounter weekend, and I attended. Frankly, I don't remember much from that weekend, but the last session is embedded in my heart. They erected a large wooden cross in the front of the stage and invited us to write on a piece of paper the one thing God was telling us to give over to Him. We were to figuratively and literally nail it to the cross.

I remember thinking and thinking what that would be. I hadn't felt Him say anything specific to me about this, so I asked God. Standing there, I said, "God, I'm sure there are a lot of things I need to totally give over to You, but what do You want me to focus on today?" I thought of my children. I think most moms' thoughts immediately go to their children when they think of what they need to "let go and let God," to use a famous cliché. But then it was as clear as a bell to me. That's the way God speaks to me. A thought just comes out of the blue.

It's usually a thought I wouldn't have had on my own, and it is consistent with His Word and His character. That's how I'm sure it's Him. The one thing I needed to nail to the cross—thus, give over to God completely—was my children's *faith*.

They were all young men now. We had done the job of raising them in the faith of our loving God. Now they needed to make choices. They needed to own their faith. I was called to *pray* but not *worry* over their decisions. My thoughts went back to when God picked me up and literally took me out of the country in order to deal with Graham. Although I thoroughly enjoyed my visit to Cabo, I didn't want God to have to deal with me first every time He wanted to deal with my children. I needed to choose to get out of the way. I could clearly see God in their lives as I looked back in time. I wanted to trust Him and move so He wouldn't have to move me. As much as I desired to do this, I wanted it to be a real decision I made and kept, not just an action I performed and one day forgot.

The more I spoke with God about it, the more faith consumed me. I wanted every one of my children to realize what I realized when Dad went to California and visited Graham. *When their Dad is present, they don't need anything else.* I'm speaking of their Heavenly Dad, God the Father. When God shows up and speaks affirmation to us, we are comforted. We experience peace and hope because He alone is peace and hope in Person. When the Heavenly Father spends time with us, we know it. He changes everything. I recently heard a truth that is still ringing in my ears: *chaos is eradicated in His presence.* Amen! That's right. When God shows up and we cooperate, then everything changes. That's what I want for my children. That's what I want for *me*. I want God to show up and for me to get out of the way and then watch everything change. Hopelessness becomes hopefulness. Anxiety becomes peace. Hatred is changed to love. The lost are found. Chaos is eradicated.

I quickly grabbed a piece of paper and pen and wrote, "Graham's faith, Jake's faith, Titus's faith, Blake's faith." I walked up to the cross, hammer in hand, and deliberately, prayerfully nailed my children's faith to the cross. By God's grace, I will never take that back. I want more for them than I could possibly give them. I want them to know what it's like to hear God's voice and feel God's presence. I'm convinced that is harder to do if my voice is ringing in their ears and I'm butting in where I don't belong.

Quickly I realized the letting go of my children's faith meant freedom for me as well. I didn't have to shoulder the burden of their belief or denial. I wasn't responsible. I could enjoy my own relationship with God. I wanted to focus on Him and Him alone. I longed to relish His lavish love over me.

Not long after that, Titus was telling me something about one of his brothers who wasn't complimentary of faith. I looked at him and said, "One thing I've realized, Ty, I'm focused on God. I'm going to heaven, and I sure hope ya'll make it." A shocking statement, I know. But he understood. We laughed together, but I know we both also said a prayer for his brother.

CHAPTER 14

The Carnival

I am comforted by the fact that we are on a journey. Our whole lives we are participating in a process. We won't be perfect until heaven. That tells me that God still loves me and walks with me when I fail. Sometimes I fail accidently, and sometimes I fail intentionally. That is true of our children as well. We wish they would learn from our mistakes. We know that's not going to happen. We didn't learn from our parents' mistakes any more than we will have faith just because our parents had faith. It is all about personal experience, personal choice, and our personal journey. I do wish Graham had made many different choices; for that matter, I wish I had made different choices, but we are each traveling down our own paths. I'm grateful God is on the adventure with us. He promises He will never leave us nor forsake us.

Graham's road continued to go up and down just like a roller coaster. By this time in life, I was very happy to have some ups along with the downs. Graham was receiving his government check monthly, and it paid the bills. However, Graham wanted to do more than pay his bills. He wanted to work. Graham's desire to be a productive member of society made me very happy. I wasn't sure where he would be able to find work. He had a criminal record, and because of his Asperger's, he remained a little awkward socially. Graham's love of computers would hopefully be his saving grace. Maybe he would get computer work where he could do the job from home. He would enjoy that.

Since Dad's visit several months earlier, Graham had been doing well. One day, Graham called saying he had a job and he would start the next day. Great news, right? Graham had landed a full-time job in a traveling carnival! This was not exactly the type of job I had in mind. I wasn't keen on Graham shacking up with a bunch of roadies. It also seemed to me that drugs might be prevalent in this type of environment. Once again, come on, Jesus! I was understandably concerned that Graham would fall back into his old bad habits if he became surrounded by people who engaged regularly in those same things.

Graham continued to tell me how he felt God around him. He spoke of an outdoor Amish church meeting he attended where God reached down and touched him in a powerful way. I felt like I was receiving mixed messages from him. I wondered if Graham's faith would ever resemble a traditional faith in any sense. My strongest thought at this point was to hang on for the next Graham ride. I encouraged myself with truth: *Keep looking up at the Author and Perfector of your faith, Lore.*

For the next three months, Graham worked at the carnival on the set-up-and-tear-down crew. He worked hard physically and was consistently paid. I didn't ask about the drug use. I didn't want to know. Graham did keep regular contact with us. We talked by phone at least once a week. His conversation was always engaging, which hadn't necessarily been the case in the past. I was encouraged that Graham continued sounding different than he had before. He seemed happy, as if he wasn't dealing with as much anxiety. I began to hang up my ideals of what my children were supposed to do or be like. I was along for the ride, praying all the way that Graham would see God's hand in his life and follow after Him, whatever that meant for him. I must admit it was fun telling people who asked about him that he had taken a job with a traveling carnival. I mean, who does that? My son does that.

After Graham's typical three-month time period, he became disenchanted with the carnival and quit. This was a relief for me. Now I was hoping he would return to his church in Sacramento. Let's turn this carnival page and make it history. However, he had a girlfriend in the carnival whom he cared for deeply.

Graham was begging this girl to leave the carnival to be with him, but she would not. Within a day or two of his phone call informing me he had quit, Graham was calling again with news that he had been rehired at the carnival. Surprised, I asked, "Graham, you hated the carnival. Why did you go back?" After a long silence, Graham managed to tell me his girlfriend was pregnant. He was determined to do the right thing, earn a living, and stay with her. I am proud that my son wanted to take care of his responsibility. I just wasn't convinced it was really *his* responsibility. There was a distinct possibility that the ex-boyfriend was the father. I was very happy she was not considering an abortion. I had learned by now things could always be worse and to look at the positives. Graham had managed to put me in a head-reeling spin again. Was I really going to be a grandmother? Could they take care of a baby? Would Michael and I end up parenting our grandchild? Would I be starting over with another Graham? I knew those conversations and answers would come in time. Focusing on God's goodness, I told Graham and myself, "This baby was thought of by God before the creation of this world. He/she is loved and wanted and has a purpose and a plan. This baby is a miracle, a blessing, and a gift from God."

By now, I was riding the Graham coaster fairly well. My self-talk sounded like this: *Hang on and look up. Hang on and look up. Things will change before you know it.* It wasn't long before that was true. After about a month, Graham quit the carnival again. He just couldn't stand the atmosphere. However, Graham would not leave his girlfriend and baby. He traveled where the carnival went but kept his distance. The carnival boss didn't want Graham coming around. He told the other young men working the carnival to keep an eye out for Graham. If they saw him, they were to threaten him. If that wasn't successful in making him leave, they were to physically hurt him. After a couple of weeks of following the carnival around, he was beaten up several times. It was at this time the girl began recanting her story. She wasn't concerned for Graham's safety, and she stated the baby wasn't his but a fellow she dated right before Graham. This devastated him. Graham still believed he was the father. He had deep feelings for this girl and was hoping that his constant care would turn her back to him. He stopped chasing the carnival but tried to keep in contact with her.

Graham went back to Sacramento and was staying temporarily with a friend from the church. He talked about staying there, but he didn't want to stay. During this time, Graham called me and said, "I feel like God is calling me somewhere, but I'm not sure where. I thought it was back to Portland where you and Dad had sent me to rehab. I'm thinking maybe I need them, but also I could work there. I called them, and they said I couldn't come back. I don't know what to do."

This is where God whispered to me, "Don't tell him what to do. You don't even know what he ought to do. Trust Me with Graham. Encourage him to follow Me." I wondered how I would do that. Graham and I talked about what it was that made him feel like God was calling him somewhere. We talked about prayer a bit. If he truly felt God leading him to Portland, then I encouraged him to go to Portland and talk with them in person. That's not really what I wanted, but he needed to listen to God for himself. I needed to trust God in Graham. Then I remember thinking about this wonderful worship music that I had recently started listening to and loved. I told Graham, "I've heard of a great church in Northern California where they have awesome worship music. I've often said when I visit California, I'm going to go visit this church." That was all that was said. Graham asked, "Where is this church?" I answered, "Redding." And with that, Graham stated, "I guess I'm going to Redding."

It was never so easy to get Graham to do something. The thing is, though, I wasn't trying to get him to go to Redding. It was just a conversation. I was at total peace trusting God was working in Graham, and now he was going to a church that was well-known for seeing God move in miraculous ways. This is the place I would love to see Graham call home. But would he really go?

CHAPTER 15

A New Life

I wasn't convinced Graham would actually go to Redding. I knew anything could happen, and like a squirrel, he might be running off to the next thing that caught his attention. However, as God would have it, a few days later, Graham called and told me he had arrived in Redding. What really surprised me was that he had also made it to church. His exact description of the time there was, "Epically awesome!" Wow. I was once again in shock with Graham, but this time, it was a wonderful shock. I had never heard Graham describe anything as "epically awesome." Could we truly be experiencing the last piece of the pie for Graham? Could this be the moment God had spoken to me about years ago when He told me Graham was going to get it? Time would tell.

He managed to get work with this older fellow he met at the local home-improvement store in exchange for a place to stay and a few meals. Graham continued to attend church and make all the meetings he possibly could. God gave him great friends who cared for him, accepted him as he was, and pointed him to Jesus. I was in grateful awe of what was happening. Through every conversation I had with Graham, I began to see him dedicating all his time to experiencing God. He had a group of friends whom he played with, experienced God with, and trusted. I was convinced Graham was beginning to grow in maturity and in his faith. We talked every few days. Our conversations were consumed with Jesus. Graham conveyed to me his experiences of the Holy Spirit speaking to him and loving him. Graham was beginning to encourage me in the Word of God.

He continued staying with this fellow Bill. After a couple of months, Graham quit working for him and began paying him rent from his monthly check. He now had a stable place to live. At the time of this transition, Bill and Michael spoke over the phone in order to work out the monthly rent and process of payment. One such conversation between Michael and Bill led to Bill telling the story of how he came to ask Graham into his home. This story is yet another example of how God takes care of us. We can trust Him with our lives and our children's lives. Bill told Michael when he went to the store that day in July, he was purchasing yard supplies to spruce up his lawn. Graham approached him and helped load his car. Graham asked him if he had any work for him. Bill didn't want to take a stranger home, so he said no but offered Graham money for loading his car. Graham declined the money, stating, "I didn't do anything to deserve being paid. Thank you." Graham went about to ask another customer for work, and Bill drove home. Bill explained to Michael, "All the way home, I couldn't get this kid out of my mind. I have never done this before, but I turned around and drove back to the store to find him and offer him work." He did find Graham. Graham accepted yard work in exchange for dinner. More work turned into a place to spend the night. Bill explained to Michael that he saw a decent young boy who needed help and help that he could provide, so he did just that. Bill had never done such a thing before and didn't really understand why he gave Graham a chance, but he did it.

I know God was looking out for Graham, and He worked through Bill to take care of him—once again, proof that Momma doesn't have to orchestrate and control the outcome of situations. Our God is intimately involved in our lives. He knows our needs and cares for us. Graham was finally ready to slow down, listen, and receive from His Heavenly Father.

It's been two years since Graham arrived in Redding, and he is still living with Bill. In fact, Bill has rented out another room to a young man who goes to church with Graham. Graham has become an emotionally, mentally, and spiritually stable young man. He continues to not only be actively involved with his church family, but Graham was also accepted as an intern in the church's ministry school. Graham is attending a local community college full-time and is making a 4.0. He calls us every week to say "I love you." He is different person. He is a new creation in Christ.

Graham is a walking miracle. Sometimes miracles happen instantaneously. Sometimes we see God's hand through medicine and the care of therapists and psychiatrists. Sometimes the miracle comes through a journey. I always want an instant miracle. Bam! Everything is inexplicably and wonderfully different. However, I am so thankful that God chose a journey for us. It's because of this hard road we have traveled that I have to depend on Christ with a deeper faith and more intimate relationship with Him. God wants to use everything in our lives to draw us into more intimacy with Him. I've discovered that I can trust Him with all that happens in my life and in my children's lives. That doesn't mean it's easy, but I'm learning to rest in the eye of the storm around me.

I can look back over my journey and see that it is God's presence that brought me peace and joy. I know this because I was experiencing peace and joy with Him before Graham was in his new life. It is not my children's circumstances that should dictate my peace and joy. If that were the case, then when things turn bad again, I would inevitably lose my peace. It's the presence of the Heavenly Father in my life that dictates my inner rest. The Person of Christ is Himself peace. When I choose to be with Him, I step into His peace like stepping into a strong tower and closing the door. No matter what kind of storm is raging outside, I have peace in Him, alone. Situations will change with me and with every one of my children. I must keep my eyes, my hope, my focus on the One who never changes, my Peace, my Jesus.

When Graham was very young, I remember telling our pastor's wife I didn't know how to teach compassion to him. Graham had an extreme personality that needed to be molded in the right direction. Today he is still extreme. Graham is now extreme for Jesus. Whatever Graham puts his mind to doing, he does it wholeheartedly. The compassion he has for people is evident to all. It is not unusual for Graham to stop wherever he is if he notices someone in need to ask them if he can pray for them. That is understandable when you consider the depths from which God has rescued Graham. He knows he has been rescued and wants to see others choose Christ and be rescued as well. He has an anointing to pray for and impart healing to others who are on the margins of society and who need a Savior. Graham's compassion has spilled over to me as well. I see the homeless in a new light. I see the mentally ill in a new light. I see that mom struggling with her disruptive child in a new light. They all need to know that instead of judgment, there is nothing but grace pouring out from our Heavenly Father. Instead of judgment or fear, they should receive compassion and grace from me.

Within a year of his move to Redding, I asked Graham about medications and his marijuana use. Graham's response surprised and thrilled me. "Mom, that stuff was all counterfeit. And I've learned where there is a counterfeit, there is the *real* thing. I'm after the real thing." God never stopped chasing after Graham. Graham finally chose God. Graham chose God's healing. This is my deepest desire come true—to see my son living in and loving God's purposes for his life. The enemy of our souls had Graham engaging in many counterfeit activities. He abused many medications and drugs in order to find rest. With Christ, Graham now sleeps well every night. He would cut himself in order to find a release from his anxiety. With Christ, Graham is honestly the most peaceful person I know. Graham's reckless behavior, suicide attempts, and panic attacks were signs of his anxiety, restlessness, and feelings of worthlessness. God has changed all that. The counterfeits the enemy offered were defeated in the Person of Jesus Christ. Jesus is Graham's peace and joy. He is now living an abundant life.

Around the time of Graham's conversion, he and I were talking on the phone. Something about Branson was mentioned, and I said I didn't care to ever go to Branson again. He said, "Why?" Surprised, I asked, "You don't remember what happened to me in Branson when we were on vacation?" "Oh," he said, "I'm really sorry about that, Mom." His apology took me by surprise. I was at peace with the reality that I would never hear an apology from Graham regarding this incident. But God had done a mighty work in him. My eyes filled with tears at his sincerity. Although it was so nice to hear, it wasn't necessary for my forgiveness. I calmly told him, "Thank you for saying that, Graham. I forgave you a long time ago."

As for Graham's ex-girlfriend who was pregnant, she had a baby girl that following January and completely cut off communication with Graham. I spoke with Graham about this when the baby was about eight months old. I asked him how he was dealing with it. I told him if he was not at peace about this, he can demand a blood test and discover the truth. He would then be able to be a father or dismiss this from his mind. Graham very maturely told me, "I am at peace, Mom. I told God that if this is my child to please let me be a part of her life. If I am not her father, then I would trust God to let us move on with separate lives." He expressed such a peace that I was almost envious.

I finally did have the wonderful opportunity to visit this place of worship and my son in Redding, California. The favorite part of my trip was watching Graham dance and sing as he worshipped God. He was free at last. That boy who folded his arms, stared at the floor, and paced during worship growing up was now a man free to dance and sing. That boy who experienced such anxiety that he would cut himself and self-medicate was now a man free from any drugs and/or medications. Graham went from "flapping" to dancing because of the healing presence of Jesus. The thing that stands out to me the most is the peace Graham now exhibits. He doesn't worry about money, friends, or the future anymore. I can honestly say that Graham is the most peaceful person I have ever been around. He has been to the place of high anxiety and depression, but with Christ, he has finally found peace and joy.

As his mom, I have also been in the place of anxiety over my son's lot in life. I feared the future possibilities, and I constantly struggled for a plan of action. I had felt defeated, fearful, and depressed so many times. *But God* was faithful. He was rarely on my time frame. He rarely went with my plans. Thank God He did things on His time frame and with His plans. It was a process with Graham. It was a process with me too. God took both me and Graham from places of anxiety and sadness to a wonderful place of peace and joy. Situations will change with me and with every one of my children. I must keep my eyes, my hope, my focus on the One who never changes, my peace, my Jesus.

Graham still has Asperger's syndrome. He is still quirky. Now we embrace it. I think Graham likes that he has AS. It makes him wonderfully different. Years ago, I had hopes that my children would choose the traditional path of success. I look back and wonder what that even means now. I suppose it meant they would become a Christian early in life, stay out of trouble, be healthy, get a good education, marry a "good girl," and make a good living to go on and raise a family of their own. I would still like that path for them, but more than anything, I desire that they have an intimate walk with the Savior of their souls. To experience Jesus is to experience peace and joy and abundance. If traveling down some of these hard roads is required in order to end up with such an abundant life, well, then bring it on. I still pray Malachi 2:5–7 for each of my children. I can see how God has developed that devoted heart, truthful spirit, and godly character in Graham.

As I recall praying for Graham during all the turmoil of his teen years, I remember saying, "God, I just want him to live and be happy." God often reminds me of that prayer. I can hear Him say, "I have always had more than that in mind. I have an abundant life and joy for him." I often think of the apartment complex in Austin near Zilker Park. I had helped Graham apply for residency there, and I thought it was the perfect place for him. It was close to the park for his enjoyment and close, but not too close, to us. The bus route ran next to it. Much to my dismay, they rejected his application. They said their policy prohibited accepting those who have committed a felony within the last two years. "But it wasn't a violent felony!" I protested and even begged, but to no avail. I told God He needed to do something because this perfect opportunity was getting away. Where in the world would Graham go if he couldn't be accepted here? To this day, I will drive by this complex on my way to the park, and I feel God nudge me and say, "Perfect place, huh?" God certainly has a sense of humor. Every time, I just laugh and say, "You knew all along, God. Thank You for bringing him to a place of freedom and joy."

I can see freedom in Graham when he encounters a situation that, in the past, would have sent him into a panic attack. Now he prays and says, "God will take care of it." I hear freedom in Graham when he calls me weekly and cheerfully says, "I'm doing good. How are you?" He freely and quickly tells us he loves us. I can feel freedom exude from him when he plays around and laughs with us. I know he peacefully sleeps through the night. At worship service in church, I have seen him take off his shoes and dance like no one is watching him. Graham continues to teach me about freedom and joy. There were years I feared for Graham's life, times when I was angry with him, times I felt relief that he wasn't around. God has changed everything. God didn't just start moving in the last days of Graham's transformation. It almost annoys me when I hear people say, "God is going to do something." I say, "God is already doing something. You just can't see or understand it yet." God was moving all along, even when things were bad. He worked it all out over several years and through some very scary and hard times. God has not wasted a single thing. He has taken all of Graham's ashes, all the things that were meant to destroy him, and turned them to beauty.

When I visited Graham, it was a joy to see him living his life and being happy. After being home a week or so, he called, and we talked for a while. At the end of the conversation, I surprised myself and very naturally said, "Okay, I'll talk with you later, my friend." Graham is now my friend. What God has done is nothing less than amazing.

Christmas 2014. Graham, Jake, Titus, Blake, Lore and Michael

It has been a tough road. If I could go back in time, naturally I would do some things differently. Looking back now, I would not have started Graham on medication so early and so quickly. I would have tried other avenues first. I wish we had taught Graham to run to Jesus first for solutions, for life change. But overall, I would travel these roads all over again to see Graham living in abundant freedom and joy. I would do it all over again to enjoy the intimacy I now feel with God. As I look over this part of our journey, I can see how God has used Graham and all my children to bring me to a place of more abundant freedom and joy. I am learning to focus on Christ, not my circumstances. I'm learning to worship in times of trouble. I am learning to believe God's promises. I am learning to trust Him in all things and through all things. I am learning to leave my baggage behind on the path that the Lord has given me to travel. Because when it comes down to it, all I need along the way, all that my kids need, all that any of us needs as we go, is Jesus.

About the Author

Lore Cottone was born and raised in Kentucky. Although her family attended church, she was the first of her family to begin a personal relationship with Christ. When she was thirteen years old, Lore gave her life to Christ at a church camp. She attended Liberty University and pursued a masters degree in social work from the University of Kentucky. Lore enjoyed working in the field of social work before marrying the love of her life, Michael, and having children. Lore and Michael have been married twenty-five years and have four sons—Graham, Jake, Titus, and Blake.

When children came along, Lore was blessed to be able to stay at home with them for almost eighteen years. Lore then reentered the social-work field for several more years until the Lord called her out to write a book about raising her oldest son. It is Lore's great hope that God will use their story to comfort and inspire many. Michael and Lore now live in Dripping Springs, Texas, and attend One Chapel church in Austin, Texas. Lore loves any physical activity outside and is a self-professed gym rat. Just don't ask her to run a marathon. Fitness classes, hikes in the great outdoors, and obstacle-course races are always on the top of her list.

For more information about the author and how to schedule Lore to speak at your next event, please visit www.lorecottone.com.